unlock your confidence workbook

Copyright © 2023 by Ellen Reimer
Kelowna BC Canada

All rights reserved. No part of this publication may be reproduced, distributed, or transmitted in any form or by any means, including photocopying, recording, or other electronic or mechanical methods, without the prior written permission of the publisher, except in the case of brief quotations embodied in critical reviews and certain other noncommercial uses permitted by copyright law.

For permission requests, write to the publisher, addressed "Attention: Permissions Coordinator," at the link below.
https://www.inspiredcounselling.ca/contact

Ordering Information:
Quantity sales. Special discounts are available on quantity purchases by corporations, associations, and others. For details, contact the publisher at the link above.

Every effort has been made to cite, acknowledge, trace or contact all copyright holders. The publisher/author will be pleased to make good any omissions or rectify any mistakes brought to their attention at the earliest opportunity.

The author is providing this book and its contents on an "as is" basis and make no representations or warranties of any kind with respect to this book or its contents. The publisher author disclaims all such representations and warranties, including but not limited to warranties of healthcare for a particular purpose. In addition, the author assumes no responsibility for errors, inaccuracies, omissions, or any other inconsistencies herein.

The content of this book is for informational purposes only and is not intended to diagnose, treat, cure, or prevent any condition, illness or disease. You understand that this book is not intended as a substitute for consultation with a licensed practitioner. Please consult with your own physician or healthcare specialist regarding the suggestions and recommendations made in this book. The use of this book implies your acceptance of this disclaimer.

The author makes no guarantees concerning the level of success you may experience by following the advice and strategies contained in this book, and you accept the risk that results will differ for each individual.

The testimonials and examples provided in this book show exceptional results, which may not apply to the average reader, and are not intended to represent or guarantee that you will achieve the same or similar results.

For general information on our other products, resources and services or to obtain technical support, please contact us at the link below;
https://www.inspiredcounselling.ca/contact

Printed Canada
Unlock Your Confidence Workbook
ISBN 978-1-7388453-2-3
Self Published
First Paperback Edition 2023
https://www.inspiredcounselling.ca/

Editor: Brittany Gale
Portrait Photo by Jenna Gibbs Photography
Illistrations used under licence from Canva

A WORKBOOK DESIGNED
TO:
EMBRACE YOUR MESSY
UNLOCK YOUR GREATEST
POTENTIAL
BE BOLD & LIVE FULLY
ALIVE

unlock your confidence workbook

Ellen Reimer RPC. CLC

acknowledgements

My life as it is would not be possible without the amazing humans that have been a part of my life, whom I'd like to acknowledge and thank
.

First, I'd like to thank my four sons for your unwavering belief in me and encouraging me to continue. You have taught me so much since the day you each were born. "I love you each so much".

I thank my dearest friends for continued encouragement, support, care, constructive criticism and love as I applied each of the tools in this book to my own life as I took my own healing journey.

I thank my extended family and friends for your heartfelt support, advice, perspectives, friendship, and walking the meandering path of life with me.

I thank the counselors and coaches in my life (you know who you are) for your support, encouragement, listening ear, inspiration, sincerity, patience, prayers and dedication to my healing journey. For the tools you have provided to me for getting me to where I am today.

Finally, I'd like to thank you, my cherished readers. To have the words of this workbook brought to life in your own healing journey is humbling, an honor, rewarding and a gift beyond measure.

Thank you from the bottom of my heart. I am genuinely and forever grateful!

welcome

about

This book is designed to promote healing into the painful places of your heart, unpack what holds you back from living your best life, find forgiveness, accept your messy and live your one and precious life with boldness!

This course will walk you through steps of **self-discovery and acceptance** for who you are and for your story.

Each chapter is built on the next, created to encourage reflection, healing, courage and hope. You will begin a journey of self reflection, processing negative core beliefs and where they originated from, walk a journey of forgiveness and explore the unique gifts, strengths and beauty created within you

The tools used in this workbook have been used by Ellen personally in her own journey to healing. Her hope is that you also will find healing, joy, hope and live your life on purpose, FULLY ALIVE!

content

1. Introduction
2. Younger You
3. Belief Debunker - Redesign Your Thoughts
4. Architect Of Your Story
5. Power In Forgiveness
6. Designing Your Road-Map
7. Life Compass - Your Core Values
8. You Shine - Strengths
9. Mining Deeper For Gold
10. Beautiful Authentic You

A message from the author

"Do you ever feel like life is just painful or hard? Maybe messy is a better word to describe it?

I know I have felt that way in my life, my description of it would be painful, hard, messy, really messy sometimes, or a lot of the time stuck...very stuck.

So I personally went on a journey to get unstuck...and even that was messy as I processed pain and heart ache and lots of tears.

As you go on this step by step journey of exploring your blocks and limiting beliefs, my hope is that you will find healing and discover the amazing and beautiful human you were created you to be.

Unlock Your Confidence is designed to help you embrace your messy, unlock your greatest potential and know the uniqueness and boldness that lies within you. You will spend the next few weeks unpacking what holds you back, the negative stories you tell yourself and will be guided through a process of self-discovery and self-acceptance for you and for your story, gaining hope and tools for overcoming negative self-talk.

You will kick low-self esteem in the butt, grab a hold of boldness and confidence as you come to know the great potential that lies within you.

You are embarking on a journey that will bring healing and wholeness, unlock the greatness within you and allow yourself to begin joyfully living the wild and precious life you have been given.

You will discover the confidence to let your true self shine and gain the keys that create personal breakthrough, healing, wholeness and live FULLY ALIVE! FULLY ALIVE!

This workbook is designed to be processed over 10 weeks - I encourage you to take the time to reflect and process each exercise as they are placed here for a purpose and reason. Each week you will take another step toward healing and gaining a deeper understanding of yourself and who you are designed and created to be.

You may also enjoy taking this journey with a friend or in a group for added support and accountability.

I know that my personal journey was not always easy... yes, there were lots of messy and hard days, but I am so grateful I took the steps towards healing and that is my hope for you. To learn who you really are, that beautiful and amazing heart and soul that you have and let the boldness that you may have hidden away have a chance to be seen. To turn your messy into a message of hope and joy."

My hope and wish for you is that the next few weeks of reflection and looking inward are insightful, healing and a time to gain a deeper understanding of the greatness within you.

Love,

Ellen

"Why are you trying so hard to fit in when you were born to stand out?"
Oliver James

quote of the day

CHAPTER ONE
introduction

WHO AM I?

Have you ever asked yourself Who AM I? Have you wondered why you are here on this earth and longed for a deeper knowing of yourself? Have you sensed there is more to life and it is just out of reach?

This course will walk you through steps of self-discovery and acceptance for who you are and for your story. Our stories do not need to define us but they do help to shape us. Discover your strengths and the beauty that lies within you.

Life has painful moments from childhood, teen years or adulthood, that can leave you feeling crushed, overwhelmed with memories and emotions, a lack of direction and purpose and feelings of being stuck forever in a limiting pattern.

I too have been there. I clearly recall the day I stood in my kitchen with tears streaming down my cheeks and cried out 'who am I?".

Many of the steps in this program have been powerful tools in overcoming my own insecurities and lack of identity. I understand the deep need to know who we are at the core of our being. I promise you also can experience the joy and empowerment in being okay with you, in knowing your worth and value and that your uniqueness is beautiful and needed in this world.

Is it easy? No, it is not, but the fact that you are here tells me that you have a desire and are ready for the steps it takes.

The only person who can change your life is you and it's going to require effort.

But the effort is worth it.

The questions below are strategic, personal and powerful to begin the process of discovering more about yourself. We often live in autopilot, without tuning in to questions and details about ourselves. Enjoy this exercise, there are a lot of questions, don't stress over the questions but rather approach them with a curiosity for yourself.

GETTING TO KNOW YOU

1. What 5 words describe you the best?

2. What are you good at?

3. What makes you happy?

4. What makes you sad or angry?

5. What is your energy drainer and makes you tired?

6. What scares you the most in life?

7. What are your hobbies?
   What are hobbies that you have dreamt of doing but have not started yet ?

8. 5 words your friends or family use to describe you?

9. What are your negative habits?

10. What are you most proud of in life?

11. What are your top 3 achievements in life?

12. What are your top 3 disappointments in life?

13. Who inspires you?

14. Using 5 words, who do you want to be in life?

15. What is the most important thing in my life?

16. Who are the most important people in my life?

17. What's my definition of success?

18. How do I want others to see me?

19. What is one dream you have that you have never shared with anyone?

REFLECTION

What insight did you gain about yourself that surprised you while answering the above questions?

Did you discover anything new about yourself?

How does it feel to discover and reflect on yourself?

HOW SELF-AWARE ARE YOU?

Part of this journey is developing self-awareness. Self-awareness allows for you to be more in tune with your beliefs, thoughts and actions.

You have the ability and willpower within you to choose and to raise your awareness levels. Raising your awareness levels will bring more clarity, authenticity, vulnerability, beauty and courage to your personal, spiritual, business/career life as well as in your relationships. Raising your awareness will require persistence and patience with yourself. It is a lifelong journey of continuing to work the self-aware muscle and having a willingness to grow and a curiosity for life.

Self-awareness is key to personal growth and discovering deeper meaning and more about yourself. Greek philosopher Aristotle expressed it this way –

"Knowing yourself is the beginning of all wisdom."

Self-Awareness is important but is also one of the most difficult skills to master and there is no one secret answer that is going to work for everyone as 'a one size fits all'. Everybody is different and you are going to be your best teacher in developing self-awareness.

It's called self-awareness for a reason. It's about you. It's about getting to know yourself on a deeper level. It's about getting really curious about who you are as a person.

What does self-awareness mean to you?

You're uncovering the things about yourself that are going to help you grow as a person and which things are harmful and damaging to you as a person.

One of the ways to become more self-aware is mindfulness.

I have struggled with the word mindfulness and with practicing it, however, I find it to be a very beneficial and important part of my everyday life for self-awareness and personal growth.

Let's take a moment to focus on mindfulness and do a body scan relaxation check. Research suggests that meditation promotes self-awareness, encouraging self-acceptance and compassion towards yourself.

MINDFULNESS EXERCISE

• Find a space that is quiet and comfortable. Put on some relaxing music if you choose.

• Begin by bringing your attention into your body.
• You can close your eyes if that's comfortable for you.
• Notice your body seated or lying down, feeling the weight of your body on the chair,
the bed or the floor.

• Take a few deep breaths.
• And as you take a deep breath, bring in more oxygen and picture yourself in your favorite place, (nature, a quiet room). And as you exhale, let your body relax more deeply.

- Notice your feet, notice the sensations of your feet touching the floor. The weight and pressure, hot or cold sensations, the vibrations

- Notice your legs - pressure, pulsing, heaviness, lightness.
- Notice your back against the floor, chair or bed.
- How does your stomach feel? Is it tense or tight, let it soften? Take a breath. Notice the rise and fall of your stomach as you continue to breath in and out.
- Notice your hands. Are your hands tense or tight? Can you let your hands loosen their grip and soften?
- Feel any sensation in your arms.
- Let your shoulders be soft.
- Notice your neck and throat. Let them be soft. Relax.
- Soften your jaw. Let your face and facial muscles soften.
- Then notice your whole-body present. Take another deep breath.
- Be aware of your whole body. Take a deep breath. When you are ready, you can open your eyes and bring your awareness back to the room.

What do you notice? Do you feel any difference? Do you feel more present and aware?

This takes patience and practice. The benefits of daily relaxation and/or mediation are great and definitely worth the time. Take time to tune into you, and into your surroundings. I have many times done a quick check-in while in nature walking or hiking.

- Pause
- Take three deep breaths
- Focus on your 4 senses, one at a time
    - What do I feel?
    - What do you see?
    - What do I smell?
    - What do I hear?

Chapter 1 | Introduction

This short exercise calms the mind and brings me back into awareness and grounds me.

During the time we are together for this course I would like to encourage you to practice mindfulness every day. Rate yourself today at the beginning of the course of how mindful and aware you feel, how present you feel and at the completion of our time together, practicing every day, rate yourself again and notice any changes that may have occurred.

Not Present All   Somewhat Present   Fully Present & Aware
1_____5_____10

LIFE INVENTORY

In the following exercise, picture each line / scale as a ladder in your life. This is not a time for you to judge yourself but rather to just become aware of all the specific areas of your life. **Awareness opens the door to change and to growth.** What we do not know, we cannot change, where there is not change, there is not growth. Awareness and change is an opportunity for growth and **a life of thriving and joy.** In the line / scale, mark where you feel you are today, not where you want to be. But where you are currently.

Relationships - how satisfied are you with the relationships in your life? (Friendships, romantic, family)
1_____10

Environment - Your physical surroundings (where you live, neighbors, relatives, colleagues)
1_____10

Career - How satisfied are you with your job, profession, business, (the way you earn an income)
1_____10

Money - Income, Expenses, Savings and Investments
1_____10

Personal Growth - how satisfied are you with the time you spend on self-development? (time you spend on continued education, reading, open mindedness, coaching, counselling)

1_____10

Enjoyment/brightness of life - what is the level of enjoyment you get from life? (pleasure, relaxation, hobbies, travel, entertainment)

1_____10

Spirituality / Faith - How satisfied or content are you with your spiritual life? (your relationship with Jesus, the time you take be with Him, how known you feel by Him) Healthy - how is your satisfaction with your health? (mental/emotional, physical, exercise, energy, nutrition)

1_____10

Reflect for a moment as you observe where you are on each ladder. Are you thriving or surviving? Are there areas of your life that you would like to change to begin thriving in this area?

Everything is interconnected. When one category suffers the others suffer. Finding a balance in each area of your wheel of life will bring you a real sense of fulfillment and wellbeing.

My hope is that throughout this course, your life will become balanced and full. Approaching life with curiosity and attention will be a game changer for you.

During the rest of the course, have a curiosity for you...

...a curiosity for the amazing and beautiful human being that you are.

I look forward to spending the next few weeks with you as you delve into exploring and discovering more about your true self. Invite compassion and curiosity as your constant companions into unlocking the greatness that lies within you.

SELF-CARE

What does self-care mean to you?

Part of self-care is self-compassion and curiosity. This week get curious, about what you love to do, what brings you joy, what makes you laugh...and then go do it.

HOMEWORK

Find an accountability partner for this journey that you have begun.

It is easy to give up the journey, feel afraid of the discomfort of unfamiliar emotions or to just need a friend / mentor to process out loud to. Find someone that you trust and feel safe with, invite them on this journey with you and to hold you accountable to continue when the going gets tough. Find someone that will listen when you need a listening ear and will encourage and support you.

Once we believe in ourselves, we can risk curiosity, wonder, spontaneous delight, or any experiences that reveals the human spirit." - E.E. Cummings

*"You are the one that possesses the keys
to your being. You carry the passport to your own happiness."
-Diane von Furstenberg*

CHAPTER TWO

younger you

GROUNDING EXERCISE

Find a space to relax and get comfortable - put some meditation music on to still your heart, mind and soul.

- Pause
- Close your eyes
- Picture a peaceful place, either in real life or an imaginary place in your mind.
- Take five deep breaths *(with each inhale, breath in the peace, with each exhale, picture the stresses of the day leaving your body)*
- Focus on your 4 senses, one at a time
    - What do I feel?
    - What do you see?
    - What do I smell?
    - What do I hear?

Notice how you feel after you have completed this grounding exercise. Notice the muscle tension, has it been released? This breathing exercise is meant to ground you in preparation for today's module.

SONG OF THE DAY

Before we delve into the next segment - prepare your heart for more by listening to music. Below is a song that has been chosen for you. Be still and let the music and words speak to you.

You Are Loved - Stars Go Dim

LET'S BEGIN

You have spent some time in the introduction asking yourself some questions and gaining some knowledge about you that you maybe tend to take for granted, things you do and think without really 'thinking' about them.

But now comes the hard work, digging deeper.

Can you **give yourself permission to put away any mask** that you may have on, any pretense, and come out of hiding for this course and especially today as you look at your younger self? That younger you.

When we stay in hiding and do not acknowledge that young child, so innocent and sweet, but yet hurting, negative beliefs and behaviors continue to have power and control, holding you back from discovering **your greatness.**

When a core belief is formed as a child it becomes a filter through which all life experiences are processed through. It is like wearing a pair of glasses with a blue lens, all of life appears blue, if you wear brown lenses then the world will appear brown. Hence if you were neglected as a child and a belief was formed that you are unlovable because you were not given the loving attention you as a child needed and deserved you will go through life looking at every experience with the belief that you are 'unlovable'. You will believe that you have to be a certain way to be loved, this belief will flow into how you perceive otheres see you and how much they love you.

Thus, if you want to change your life as an adult, **it is vital to change the belief system,** the lens through which you look, finding a new core belief. To do this, it is important to connect with your younger self. That little girl or boy that you were. To grieve and to give yourself permission to grieve and experience healing.

Grieving is an important part of the journey to finding our true sense of self as we grieve the pain the younger you experienced. We cannot finish the past without the ability to grieve.

Every child needs to know that they are loved unconditionally. Loved without judgment and to know that they matter and are significant, that they can trust their caretakers and are safe.

Chapter 2 | Younger You

The Inner Child **needs gentleness and compassion** as you go on this journey through childhood memories of the heart and to connect with the child within. Picture yourself in a safe place as you walk through the memories.

How do you see this little child?

Let yourself love and be curious... have you met your inner child? Can you have compassion and curiosity for her/him? Your inner child is the t**ruest and most authentic core of your being.** The youngest and most innocent part of you that has been hidden away.

This younger version of you is also the part of you that took on beliefs about yourself that cause fear, insecurity and shame. **Every experience is shaped by those beliefs.**

When your inner child is neglected, she/he withers away, burying creativity, vitality, expressiveness and energy within. When the needs of the child are left unresolved, it is a pain, which as an adult, is then acted out, some people refer to this as the 'shadow self' or 'wounded inner child'.

When the pain of the wounded child is left unattended, you tend to bury the energy and expressiveness of the inner child, missing out on the playfulness, trust relationships, joy, belly laughs, spontaneity, bliss, awe, wonder and the soul/heart connections and instead act out of the wounded inner child or shadow self, feeling depressed, anxious, angry, frustrated, isolated, reserved, shy, alone. You may struggle with codependency, toxic relationships, unhealthy boundaries and a lack of communication skills. The effects of the wounded inner child reach far and wide into every aspect of life and will be found in many forms of pain impacting you physically, mentally, emotionally and spiritually.

The younger you simply wanted and longed **to be loved and held in a safe space** by the caretakers and most significant people in your life. And that young you is still longing to be held by love and acceptance. To be given permission to just be you.

To know that you are deeply loved and to experience the world with an openness and wonder, while having the confidence in your adult self to have the wisdom that life experiences bring.

This Journey is not easy and may be very painful for you. Have compassion for yourself and if you are not ready for this step, that is ok. Skip to the next session or

25

contact your councilor to help you work through this process. If you do not have a counsellor, Inspired Counselling & Coaching offers on-line counselling and can be contacted here: www.inspiredcounselling.ca/contact We are all on a journey and at different places of healing and it is okay to feel uncomfortable for this step.

My first step into healing my inner child and learning love and acceptance for myself as a woman was finding a picture of myself when I was 1.5 years old. Oh, the sweetness and innocence with childlike, wide-eyed wonder.

Your first step to healing in this module is to find a picture of your younger self. That little girl or little boy...the one that makes you smile with love today. The one that, if you met that little girl in the park you would want to give her a hug and tell her how adorable she is with her dimples and messy, wind-blown hair.
(I would encourage finding 2 or 3 pictures at different stages of your life. A toddler, school age and teenager.)

JOURNALING

Take some time for this exercise. Create space and time to be alone, find a place that feels safe where you can let yourself feel the emotions, put on your favorite music and let yourself relax into this time with compassion and curiosity.

Look into the eyes of that little child. What do you see? What would you say to that little girl, little boy today if you saw them on the playground or building a sandcastle on the beach? Look at the teen with curiosity and compassion, what would you say to that young teenager trying so hard to fit in?

What does that little girl need to hear from you today? How beautiful she is... how you love her spunkiness... What else?

What does the teenager, so desperately needing acceptance and validation need to hear from you?

What did she not get back then, that today you can give her? What is she longing to hear? What would make her laugh in delight?

Think about what you loved to do as a child. Take a walk down memory lane... did you like to climb trees, maybe you built tree forts. Rock collections or building towns in the sandbox. Did you enjoy riding bikes with friends, or reading a favorite story book? Did you have a favorite cuddling stuffy or a pet? What was your favorite food? Who was your favorite person? That safe place?

Allow yourself to go on a journey with your younger self by asking some questions and allowing yourself to feel the emotions and thoughts that you experience in this process. It is ok to feel messy at this time. That is why you chose a safe and quiet spot to journal this process. be patient, be loving, kind and accepting.

When was the first time you felt scared?

When did you first feel unsafe? Unloved? Lonely?

It may be easier to do an imagery walk down memory lane.

Relax, close your eyes and breathe deeply.

Imagine you're walking down a pathway through a field of grass and wildflowers. This field is a safe place where you feel loved and secure. Soak in your surroundings, what does it feel like? Smell like and look like?

Imagine a small child coming down the pathway or running through the grass towards you. This child is your younger self. You open your arms and give the small child a gentle bear hug and gently set them down beside you on a picnic blanket, maybe this young child, younger you is sitting safely tucked in your arms

When you're ready, ask the small child the questions you would like to ask?
- "When was the first time you/I felt sad or scared?"

- When did you first feel lonely? Rejected? Abandoned? neglected?

- Deep inside you, you may hear an answer, a knowing.

- Have compassion for the small child, hold him/her gently

- What would you as the adult like to say to the young child now?

- Make sure you hug them, thank them, and tell them how much they mean to you.

- Say goodbye to them.

- Leave the field of grass and wildflowers

- Open your eyes and tune into how you are feeling, the emotions and thoughts that you are experiencing.

Some places may be too painful to imagine walking into.

You may have experienced abuse, pain no child, girl or woman should ever experience. Neglect. I am sorry this has happened to you. I am sorry you did not receive the love you deserved. The safety.

Give yourself some space to acknowledge the pain, the sorrow, the anger. Can you let yourself grieve the loss or lack? It was wrong! Picture your little girl self and be compassionate with her, give her some empathy.

As adults, we view the world very differently than we did as little children. Oftentimes, what we view as insignificant as an adult was painful and left deep scars in the child. It may be a parent that was always at work, being bullied in school, an emotionally distant parent, a controlling or manipulative caregiver, adult responsibilities and worries at too young of an age, words that were not supportive, words that should have been said but were not, eg. you are beautiful, I love you, abuse - emotionally, physically, sexually, spiritually. These all, as significant or insignificant as they may seem, have an effect on our childhood and we carry this into adulthood.

These exercises are not to berate caregivers, but to bring awareness to your emotional childhood map. Through gently exploring your childhood and connecting with your younger self, you open yourself up for opportunity to grieve, beginning the healing process from pain that you have unconsciously or consciously been holding on to for years. Unmet needs and repressed childhood emotions, along with a childlike enthusiasm and innocence, creativity, playfulness, sensitivity and wonder lie within you waiting to be set free.

This journey into healing will allow you to open yourself up to claiming that part of you that has been hidden for so many years, to fully walk into your passions and live uninhibitedly. By connecting with your younger self, or inner child you connect with feelings that have been suppressed and causing challenges as an adult, bringing these feelings to awareness allows you to focus on the root cause of your challenges, insecurities, limiting beliefs and lack of self-confidence and identity.

Transformation takes place deep within us as expression and voice is given to the 'inner child' and suppressed emotions.

Journal your thoughts and your feelings. There is no right or wrong to this exercise, just give yourself permission to look at that delightful younger version of you with curiosity and love. If you are struggling to connect to this exercise... think of a young child you know today, maybe a niece or nephew, a godchild or a friend's child. What would you say to them if their story was like yours? What do they need?

JOURNAL

DIGGING DEEPER

You have taken a walk down memory lane and likely feel emotional and tired by now, wondering if this is really worth all the feels you are feeling. This has been hard and painful to remember, and yet so important. Be proud of yourself for taking this step.

We have another exercise in this session that may be hard to do. **Take a short break,** make yourself a cup of tea, or go for a short walk, then **create some time and space**.

When you are ready, and only when you are ready I am asking you to write a letter to your parents, caregiver, guardian. The adult in your life that you experienced pain from. You may need to write more than one letter. It may be to 2 or 3 individuals, but write, **UNCENSORED.**

This is not a time for politeness, this is a time **to say everything** that you did not say as a child but needed to. Everything you have wanted to say but couldn't as you were growing up. Let yourself be angry, mad, cry. Let yourself grieve what you didn't have, what you lost, the neglect or abuse, This is not a time to censor your writing, there may come a day when you want to write the letter censored but for today this one's for you to write all those suppressed emotions, feelings, thoughts on paper, to give your younger self and now adult self a chance to say what you have not been able to express. To give yourself a voice.

What came up for you during this letter writing?

Were there emotions and feelings that surprised you?

You may feel that now is a time to talk with your counsellor about the experiences and trauma you may have gone through.

Take time to ground yourself - Take 3 - 4 deep breaths, picturing a peaceful, safe place as you breathe in and the tension and negative emotions flowing out as you let go of the breath. Take note of your senses - What do you smell? What do you feel? What do you hear?

SELFCARE

Be gentle and compassionate to yourself. Self-care is vital in the healing and discovery journey you have embarked on. Take a walk-in nature or a hot bath with candles, do for you what gives you a sense of well-being.

Be proud of yourself for starting on this journey to healing and taking the difficult steps that you did today.

What will you do for selfcare today? This week?

HOMEWORK

Keep a picture of that adorable younger you on the fridge or dresser, somewhere that you can see her every day.

Throughout the duration of this course, what can you incorporate into your activities that you loved to do as a child? Or that you dreamed of doing?

You stepped outside of the comfort zone today and that is where growth takes place and change happens. I am so proud of you for being willing to go deep today!

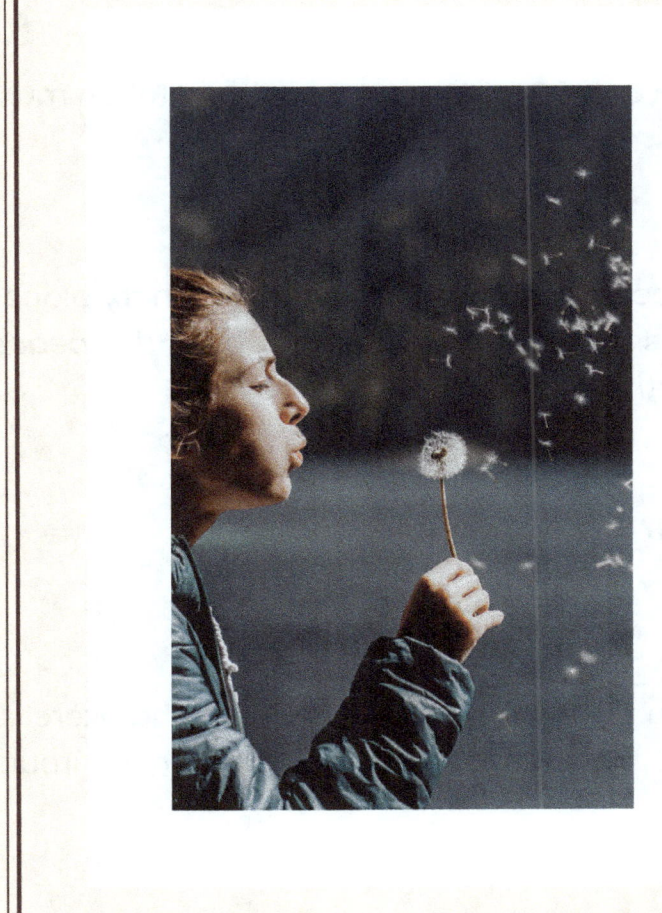

CHAPTER THREEE

redesign your thoughts

GROUNDING EXERCISE

Find a space to relax and get comfortable - put some meditation music on to still your heart, mind and soul.

- Pause
- Close your eyes
- Picture a peaceful place, either in real life or an imaginary place in your mind.
- Take five deep breaths *(with each inhale, breath in the peace, with each exhale, picture the stresses of the day leaving your body)*
- Focus on your 4 senses, one at a time
    - What do I feel?
    - What do you see?
    - What do I smell?
    - What do I hear?

Notice how you feel after you have completed this grounding exercise. Notice the muscle tension, has it been released? This breathing exercise is meant to ground you in preparation for today's module.

SONG OF THE DAY

Before we delve into the next segment - prepare your heart for more by listening to music. Below is a song that has been chosen for you. Be still and let the music and words speak to you.

Fight Song - Rachel Platten

LET'S BEGIN

"We are what we believe"
-CS Lewis

In the last segment of this program, you had the courage to meet up with your younger self, this may not have been easy for you as painful memories may have surfaced, or for some it might have been a pleasant walk down memory lane as you remembered that young child in all his/her innocent cuteness.

In this module, we are going to explore how those experiences you had as baby, child or teen created a core belief in you.

You might ask what is a core belief?

A core belief is a deep rooted,, automatic belief you have about yourself, about other people and the world you live in. These beliefs are absolute truths deep inside you, underneath all the thoughts that are surface.

Core beliefs are very convincing and full of persuasion, something that you accept as truth without question. Your mind filters and interprets the world, situations, and circumstances through this deep root effortlessly. When something happens, your mind automatically opens the door to the core belief and consults with it for advice, safety, approval, acceptance.

A core belief becomes how you see yourself, and to what degree you feel your importance is in this world, **how worthy you believe you are of love, how safe, competent, powerful and accepted you feel**. Your self-esteem is rooted in that belief.

Our experiences in life create an internal story in us that we tell over and over again and look to the world around us to confirm its truth.

When the story that has been created in us is positive, such as your parents telling you every day how beautiful you are, you are going to grow up with the belief that you are beautiful. If you grew up never hearing the words ' I love you' you may grow up with the belief that you are unlovable or unworthy to be loved.

Chapter 3 | Belief Debunker – Redesign Your Thoughts

A belief can come from childhood experiences, friendships, relationships, school years, jobs, experiences that we perceive as failures or accomplishments. There are many places that your beliefs become deeply rooted and through the years the story you told yourself confirmed the belief over and over again. Consider where the story may have come from. Are you hearing the voice of a parent from your childhood? Are you hearing echoes of a partner who pulled you down and undermined your self-esteem? In finding the origins of some of your core beliefs it can help to change them.

Dr Daniel Amen expressed:

"Your brain is always listening to and responding to these hidden influences and unless you recognize and deal with them they can steal your happiness, spoil your relationships and sabotage your health.""

Your core beliefs have a huge influence on your sense of belonging and how you perceive others view you and are treated by others.

A negative belief about yourself is destructive to your self-acceptance and self-esteem. It is like this core belief has a voice all of its own and speaks whenever it wills.

"Beliefs have the power to create and the power to destroy. Human beings have the awesome ability to take any experience of their lives and create a meaning that dis-empowers them or one that can literally save their lives."
— Tony Robbins

Most of us will battle at some point in our lives with thoughts and feelings which threaten to derail our success and happiness. Thoughts that will keep you feeling like you cannot move forward in life and will hold you back from owning who you are.

An internal judge sabotages your ability to move towards your truth and happiness. It keeps you from having compassion and gentleness with yourself.

To change the story, you are telling yourself you must first identify the belief that is limiting you and **replace it with the truth.**

You get to rewrite your story and grasp onto beliefs that are your truth.

You are the author of your story and the architect of your life experiences.

Chapter 3 | Belief Debunker – Redesign Your Thoughts

Are you ready to explore and debunk those negative core beliefs and fire the inner critic? Make a list of the areas in your life where you feel challenged and unhappy. Areas that you feel pressure or stuck and are not satisfied with. Areas that you would like to create change.

What are your goals and activities you would like to do but find a reason why you cannot do it?

Fill in the Blank

I would like to _____, but I cannot because _____.

Can you identify the belief in the above statement?

I would like a relationship, a career but I cannot because _____
_____
_____

Your behavior is an indicator of your beliefs. We do not do something because we have a limited belief.

LET'S DIG DEEPER.

Limited beliefs are often preceded by a fear.

Examples of fear:
- Fear of what others will think of me
- Fear of failure
- Fear of conflict

What do you fear the most? Take some time to reflect on the answer to this question.

Another way to discover fear is asking yourself, "What door would I walk through if I did not fear"?

If I did not fear _____,
I would do _____.

Fears and limiting beliefs walk hand in hand.

There are layers of beliefs within a thought that causes your system to create fear; there is an event or a trigger, followed by a space in which we attach to a feeling of fear that immediately attaches to a belief. This belief increases the fear and the dragons in your mind have a party while they watch you hold back from being your authentic self and go after the dreams and goals that you have..

EXPLORING

Let's identify the beliefs that are holding you back - As you look at the door that fear is holding you back from, what is the belief that keeps you from opening the door and walking through it?

What is the inner judge or dragon saying to you as you consider moving towards the door?

Which beliefs are having the greatest **negative** impact on your life?

With compassion and kindness examine the belief(s) and consider the change that your life would experience if you were not held back by that belief or if that belief were eliminated from your life.

What do the beliefs hold you back from?

"The only thing that's keeping you from getting what you want is the story you keep telling yourself." –Tony Robbins

Dr Caroline Leaf says:

"Whatever you think about the most will grow; if you are thinking about something daily, within approximately two months your brain has changed to accommodate this pattern of thought."

You create a filter or mindset through which you see life when you think about a situation constantly. You condition your mind to think a certain way. Similar to that of working out in the gym. When we work a certain muscle repeatedly it conditions your body to look a certain way, the same holds true for our minds, we condition them to filter our thoughts and beliefs through a negative or positive filter

"If you realized how powerful your thoughts are, you would never think a negative thought." Caroline Leaf,

These beliefs affect our body, soul and mind.

Do your beliefs today make you question who you are? Your judgment? Your gut instincts? Your career? Ever feel like a fraud? Shame? Guilt? Not good enough? It is as if a dragon is sitting on your shoulder and shouting, "no see, you can't do this, you are too this and too that".

Is this your truth? Or is this a story you adopted as yours? What is truth whispering to you? What is the truth wanting to say to you?

Are you going to give that dragon power or the truth? **It is your choice.**

Our beliefs about ourselves will propel us forward or hold us back. **They shape the decisions we make,,** our yes and our no, our boundaries, and the way we communicate. Our energy and the way we see ourselves.

We all have names, beliefs, lies, words we have believed. Beliefs that create a shame and/or fear within us.

Can you see we all have insecurities? We compare, we put ourselves down, we criticize ourselves and others due to our insecurities. What would it feel like to view yourself as equal to the person you so admire?

Most of us will battle at some point in our lives with thoughts and feelings which threaten to derail our success and happiness.

Do you celebrate your victories or focus on your failures? Do you look truthfully at what you are doing in your own life and what others are doing?

The comedian Irwin Corey once remarked:

"If we don't change direction soon, we will end up where we're going.'

By identifying and changing the core beliefs in our mind so many of our uncomfortable emotions and sabotaging behaviors dissolve away. **The first and most critical step in this process is to be aware**.

JOURNALING

Write a word blast, uncensored, any and all thoughts that are in your mind. Write about the dreams and goals you have and let the thoughts form words on paper read what you wrote, and observe the words with curiosity. Are they positive or negative? What beliefs about yourself can you identify in your words?

In the narrative of these thoughts, you create a story about yourselves. Do you recognize a judge in your story? Is there a victim voice (poor me) (helpless) a voice that accepts and takes on the voice of the judge? A voice that accepts the voice of the judge to be true? Do you base your identity on what the judge and victim are saying? Is there a persecutor voice that is harsh?

Here are some other examples of common core beliefs that we hide inside:
- I am irredeemably flawed.
- Something is wrong with me
- I am unlovable.
- I am bad.
- I am stupid.
- I am worthless.
- I am a loser.
- I don't deserve good things.
- I am a failure.
- I am weak.
- I am not enough.
- I don't matter.
- I am bored.
- I am crazy and unstable.
- I can't be fixed.
- I always hurt people
- I always hurt myself.
- I have no hope.
- I am bad
- I am unwanted.
- I am invisible.
- I made a mistake.
- I am helpless.
- I am ugly.
- I am shameful.
- I am uninteresting.
- I will die alone.

DEBUNKING THE BELIEF

Often, you'll discover that there is one main core belief that seems to pervade a lot of what you think, feel and do. Challenge and debunk this belief first.

The thoughts that we suppress hurt us. **Bring it out into the open as if you are going into battle with your dragon. Challenge it. Correct it**!

Write down your negative core belief (*the act of writing it down gives it less power*) You may have more than 1 belief that you want to work through this process with.

Is it true? *On a scale of 1 to 10, how much do you truly believe this belief? Rate how much conviction you have in your core belief.*

I Don't Believe At All   Strongly Believe

10 _____ 1

Ask yourself, "Why do I believe this is true about myself?"

Is it 100% true?

How do I feel when I believe this thought?

Reflect on memories or experiences that hold your belief. Identify any emotions (such as fear) hiding behind your beliefs.

How would I feel if I didn't have this thought?

EXPLORE HIDDEN FORMS OF RESISTANCE

You will need to be able to deeply commit to the journey of rewriting limiting beliefs by becoming conscious of what is holding you back from changing

Is this belief serving you today? When you can see that it is no longer being positively served by this deeply held conviction it is easier to make room for new and positive beliefs. What has long lasting (eternal) value ? Am I acting in a way that will make me proud of my life?

By managing thoughts and creating a thought routine we can debunk and redesign the thought.

>Take the original thought, turn it to the opposite, flip it. It's important that you choose a core belief that you genuinely believe in.

>Is this new belief true?

>What is the evidence of truth for this new opposite thought?

>Examine the cost and the benefit of the new belief.

>Create 2 lists. One list is the costs of having the new belief and one listing the benefits you will gain with the new belief.

>Again...What is your truth?

>What is the evidence of the truth for this new opposite thought?

Explore how your life will change with your new truth and belief.

How will your new core belief transform your life? Will it help you to be more joyful, confident, creative or prosperous?

Is this new belief in alignment with your values and create a sense of peace?

If you don't change your core beliefs, what will be the consequence?

Reflect on or write down your thoughts.

What is the evidence of truth for this new opposite thought?

What action steps can you put into place to ensure the truth becomes an automatic belief that replaces the limiting belief.

Whenever you experience a flux in emotion, **pay attention**!

Replacing your core beliefs will take time and effort, but **the rewards are endless and priceless**. Increased self-esteem, creativity, productivity, prosperity, joy, fulfillment, and love are some of the many gifts you will receive throughout this journey of rewriting your internal dialogue and story.

Look at it as washing your brain clean. We wash our bodies, hands ,hair, why wouldn't we wash our brains of toxic, negative thinking so we have clean thinking..

COACH VS JUDGE

If you think of a little child, their 'look mom look, see what I did' ' they are always looking for the coach... you are born with an inner coach that encourages and looks for the successes, over the years this voice was told to be quiet, and the judge stepped in.

Claim back and strengthen your inner greatness and coach by giving it permission to look for the truth in each thought.

Write down all your successes, your proud moments, your accomplishments. Rejoice in them, cherish them.

For each fear write an act of courage or accomplishment in your life

For each limiting belief write your truth

FOOD FOR THOUGHT

Scientifically we have 90 seconds from the time a thought enters your mind to either hook into it or to let it pass by. You get to choose whether you hook into a limiting thought or a positive thought and to tell the limiting or negative thought that you do not have space for negativity or limits and to leave.

SELFCARE

Spend some time reflecting what you have discovered today. Go for a walk in nature. Listen to your favorite playlist that motivates you.

Share your discovery with a trusted friend and ask him / her to hold you and the dragon accountable.

HOMEWORK

Picture yourself living life in your truth. What does this look like? What are you doing?

Do something that has scared you to do because you believed the judge and dragon. Journal the above exercise and how you felt doing it

"I want to be in the arena. I want to be brave with my life. And when we make the choice to dare greatly, we sign up to get our asses kicked. We can choose courage, or we can choose comfort, but we can't have both. Not at the same time." Brene Brown

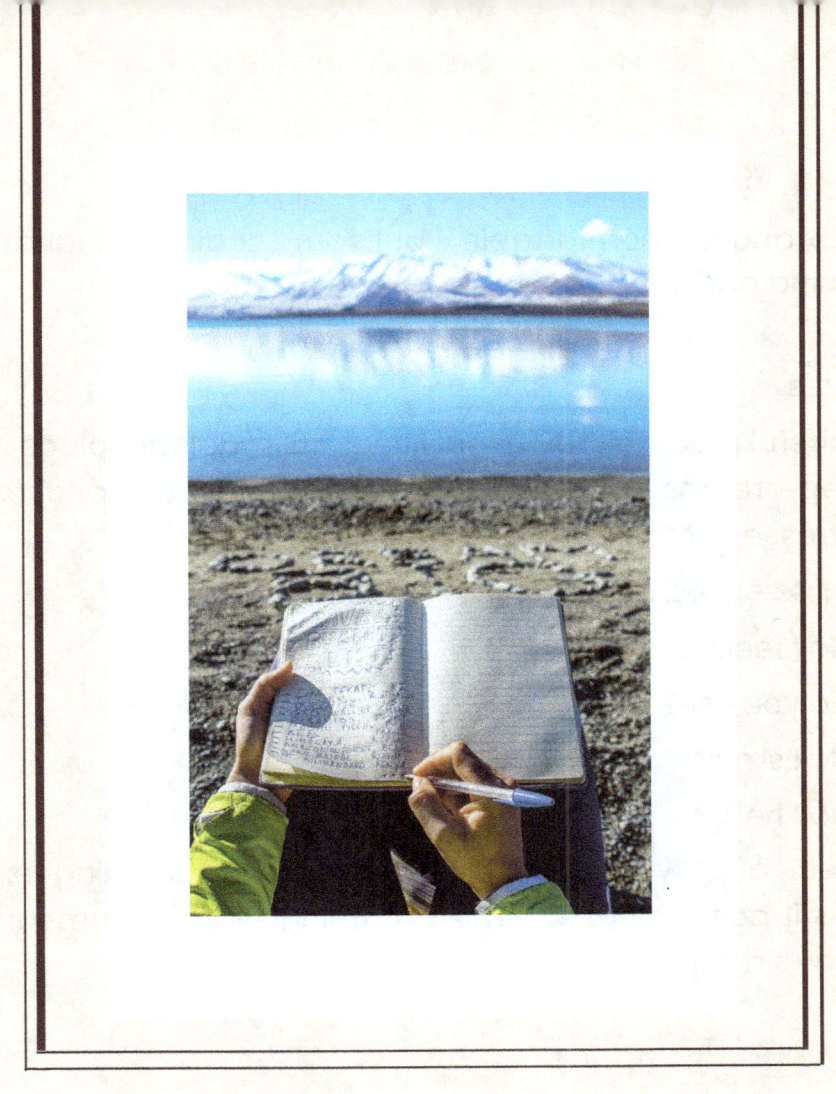

CHAPTER FOUR

architect of your story

GROUNDING EXERCISE

Find a space to relax and get comfortable - put some soaking meditation mmusic on to still your heart, mind and soul.

- Pause
- Close your eyes
- Picture a peaceful place, either in real life or an imaginary place in your mind.
- Take five deep breaths *(with each inhale, breath in the peace, with each exhale, picture the stresses of the day leaving your body)*
- Focus on your 4 senses, one at a time
    - What do I feel?
    - What do you see?
    - What do I smell?
    - What do I hear?

Notice how you feel after you have completed this grounding exercise. Notice the muscle tension, has it been released? This breathing exercise is meant to ground you in preparation for today's module.

SONG OF THE DAY

Below is a song that has been chosen for you. Be still and let the music and words speak to you.

Stronger Than Before - Olivia Newton -John

I'm Ready for a Change - Katie Drake

Chapter 4 | Architect Of Your Story

LET'S BEGIN

This segment of the course is short but thought provoking. My hope for you is that in this time you will gain a deeper understanding of yourself and your story.

Our stories do help to shape us, but they do not need to define us unless we let them.

I am going to share a little piece of my personal journey in discovering acceptance for myself and for my story.

I hated me and I hated my story!
I was great at hiding. Hiding my true self under a pretense of quiet and shy. I was scared to be seen and to be heard. I was ashamed of who I was and where I came from.

I sat one day with a coach, and he had an assignment for me that I resented and felt like it was a complete waste of my time... But... it had a profound effect on how I viewed my story..

He said *"I want you to write a letter to your 18 year old self the night before you got married"* and *"remember, you had a choice"*.

My letter was formulated in my head in a bunker, and later put on paper. I was working at a golf course at 5:30 AM. In the stillness of the morning, while raking bunkers, I found it was a great time for some deep reflection and soul searching.

That day, in the bunker, my story changed, it no longer has the power to control me or define me, but I came to the deep realization that my story shaped me and continues to shape who I am today and my future. my.

You see, I was letting my story create negative beliefs in me about who I am and what my value was based on what happened to me and around me, I believed lies about myself that led me to believe that I was unlovable, unworthy, unimportant and so many other negative beliefs. I could not accept I was worthy of love and acceptance. e.

Your story also shapes you. You have a choice at how you write your story.

We each have an opportunity to rewrite our stories.

Before you go into letter writing, take some time to reflect on the exercise below

TIMELINE EXERCISE

On a blank paper draw a timeline.

Date of birth   Present time
(0 months)   (current age)
_____

For every event that is memorable to you, mark it on the timeline. For every sad or painful event make a line downward and for every happy and positive event make a line upwards. The length of the mark will be determined by the depth of the event. *E.g., the day you got married may be a long line upwards. The day you lost a job would be a line down. The greater the loss the longer the line.*

Look at the up and down lines as your heartbeat on a heart monitor. It is your story, your pain, your joy, it is what you have experienced.

Reflect on your timeline. How does it make you feel to look at the timeline that tells a snapshot story about you?

DEAR YOUNGER ME

Listen to the song suggestion by Nichole Nordeman below before you begin this segment.
Nichole Nordeman – Dear Me

Create some time in your schedule. Find a place that is quiet and undisturbed.

Write a letter to your younger self at a pivotal point in your life.

Picture your younger self today, go for a walk with her, where you loved to go when you were young.

I found myself sitting on my bed in my childhood home with my young teen self. As I pictured myself sitting there, my heart softened, and I became compassionate for the young version of me.

Picture your younger self...what would the adult you say to the younger you?

Dear 5-year-old me
Dear 10-year-old (insert name here)
Dear 15-year-old....

You may choose to write to different ages of this young and beautiful/handsome girl/boy

Remember in life we have a choice, even when we do not feel like we do, it may be as drastic as choosing life over death. It may be the most tragic and painful moment, but you chose life, you are here today, lovely and beautiful in who you are.

Dear_____

REFLECTION TIME

How did writing this letter affect you?

What new insight did you gain?

How does it shift your perception of your story?

How does it shift the story you tell yourself about your value and worth?

How can your story be used to impact others and help make the world a better place?

What are the unique gifts and qualities that have become a part of you through your story?

What desires and dreams have grown?

Can you begin to see the shift, the 'beauty that comes from the ashes', the healing of the deep parts of your heart that have been wounded, feel the hope replace th hopeless?

If you met another woman at the coffee shop, and over a cup of spicy latte, she shared a story with you that was like your story, how would you see her? What compassion would you have for her? What would you say to her as she shares? And as she sits back in her chair with a deep sigh and a tear in her eye and says "and that is how I got here today" what would you look at her and say?

Would you look at her and say words that were harsh and judgmental or would you gently touch her hand with compassion and say 'wow, thank you for sharing, you are incredible and strong, courageous for having come through all that and be sitting here today. Your story is inspiring.

Reflect on this question and journal your answer. A beautiful woman sits across the table from you and tells you her story, which is yours. What do you say to her? What do **you** say to **you**?

JOURNAL

You are designed and created for greatness.

Like the oyster that takes sand from the bottom of the ocean, and then becomes a pearl, this too, is what your story, all the pain, hurt, tragedy and glorious moments have created in you. **A beautiful pearl!**

Your endurance, your courage. YOU! YES YOU, have an incredible story that has helped to shape you into the glorious person that you are today.

SELF-CARE

Take time this week to go for a walk - find some water to sit beside- the ocean, a lake, stream or waterfall. Get into nature and enjoy the beauty around you. Be aware of your senses as you walk, the smells, sounds and sights.

Do something for you - it may be eating an ice cream cone or going for a kayak ride or just sitting in the sun, whatever it is, do something that brings you joy in your soul.

HOMEWORK

Reread the letter you wrote to your younger self. Reflect some more on the strengths and beauty that have been instilled deep in your soul from the journey you have been on.

*"I can choose either to be a victim of the world or an adventurer in search of a treasure.
It's all a question of how I view my life."*
— Paulo Coelho

"You have to begin to tell the story of your life as you now want it to be and discontinue the tales of how it has been or of how it is."
– Esther and Jerry Hicks

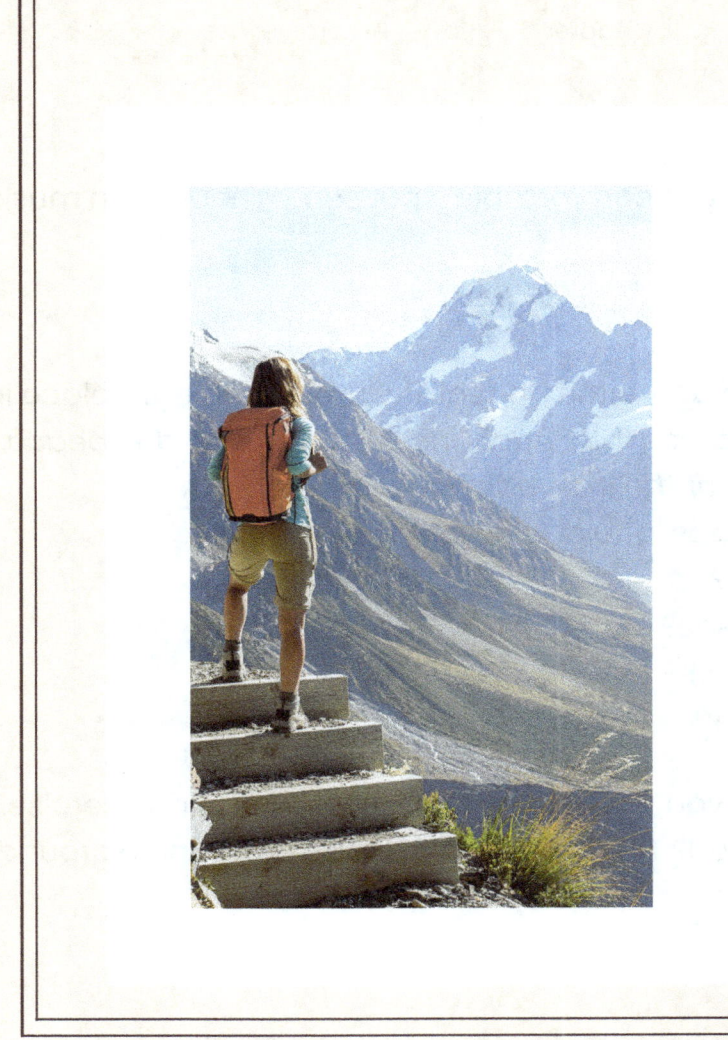

CHAPTER FIVE
power of forgiveness

GROUNDING EXERCISE

Find a space to relax and get comfortable - put some meditation music on to still your heart, mind and soul.

- Pause
- Close your eyes
- Picture a peaceful place, either in real life or an imaginary place in your mind.
- Take five deep breaths *(with each inhale, breath in the peace, with each exhale, picture the stresses of the day leaving your body)*
- Focus on your 4 senses, one at a time
    - What do I feel?
    - What do you see?
    - What do I smell?
    - What do I hear?

Notice how you feel after you have completed this grounding exercise. Notice the muscle tension, has it been released? This breathing exercise is meant to ground you in preparation for today's module.

SONG OF THE DAY

What is your heart feeling today? Below is a song that has been chosen for you. Be still and let the music and words speak to you.

Tell Your Heart To Beat Again - Danny Gokey

LET'S BEGIN

Forgiveness is at the core of healing. When you forgive, it sets you free and allows your heart to heal, opening doors to endless possibilities.

Forgiveness is not easy, nor is it always about forgiving someone else. Forgiving someone that has hurt you is vital to your wellbeing, but just as important is **forgiving yourself,** which I, personally, have often found to be the most difficult action. In this chapter, you may need to walk through forgiveness for more than one person.

When you forgive you are not excusing or justifying the actions of someone, but rather, you are **lifting the burden from your heart.**

Forgiveness stems from a deep belief **that you are enough, that you are loved** and that even though you were wronged, you don't have to spend your emotional energy trying to get revenge or have the debt paid back for the pain that was instilled on you. It takes practice to train our minds to learn the art of forgiving and letting go of what was to make room for healing and new opportunities.

"Healing and forgiveness walk hand in hand. Forgive yourself, forgive others, forgive life itself and experience a freedom, wholeness and joy deep within your heart."

Practicing forgiveness, releasing resentment, and learning acceptance is an opportunity to practice love even when it's not easy.

Forgiveness, is a form of surrender and release, expanding our capacity to love. It is setting a prisoner free. **You set yourself free when you set others free** and when you forgive yourself.

Forgiveness is a journey not a destination. Sometimes forgiveness happens in layers, and we need to forgive many times over. I would like to say that forgiveness is a 'once forgiven, all forgotten", however in our humanistic ways, we do not forget and often pick up the backpack of unforgiveness again, taking it with us through life, until we again choose to unpack the backpack and forgive. **It is a choice we get to make each day.** To forgive or to remain hurt.

Forgiveness does not mean that you let the individual hurt you again, or even that you let them back into your life. Forgiveness is an act of setting yourself free of the resentment, bitterness and pain caused by the wrongdoing and setting healthy boundaries for yourself.

Forgiveness is a choice and when we choose to forgive it brings transformation. It transforms us from victim to survivor, from helpless to empowered. **It brings freedom to our minds and hearts when we embrace opportunities to forgive.**

Forgiveness means finding the courage to see our own errors – not just those of others. It turns away the false messages of harsh self-judgment to ourselves and judgment to another.

When we choose to forgive it brings transformation. It transforms us from victim to survivor, from helpless to empowered. It brings freedom to our minds and hearts when we embrace opportunities to forgive.

REFLECTIONS FOR BLOCKS TO FORGIVING

- Do I believe that forgiving requires something of the other person first?
- Has this wrongdoing, pain and resentment become part of my identity?
- What are the pleasures of this anger and resentment?
- Is there a part of me that wants to entertain the anger?
- Is withholding forgiveness about my ego?
- What would forgiveness look like?
- Is this where I want to stay?

Reflect and journal your thoughts and emotions from the above questions.

STEPS TOWARDS FORGIVENESS

- Name the wound.

- Name the trigger.

- Name the person that hurt you.

During the uncovering phase of forgiveness, you will gain a deeper understanding of the injustice, and how it has impacted your life. Begin exploring by describing the pain you have endured.
NOTE: If you are feeling re-traumatized, do a grounding technique and enter the process slowly when you are ready or talk with a trained trauma counselor

- Remember the pain of the incident: What happened?

- What is the hardest thing to forgive?

- Why was this treatment unfair? How have the injustices affected you?

- Where do you carry this in your body?

- How long have you carried the pain?

Imagine taking it from your body and holding it in your hands. Look at it from every angle with compassion and curiosity.

The next questions may seem irrelevant, however please answer the questions quickly, without thinking deep into them.

- What color is it?

- What shape is it?

- Does it have a smell?

-Does it make a noise?

-How old is it?

Observe and look at the object you have described with curiosity. As you continue to process through forgiveness, you will come back to this object that you have described.

During the decision phase of forgiveness, you will gain a deeper understanding of what forgiveness is and make the decision to choose or reject forgiveness as an option.

Forgiveness is a choice you get to make.

You may wrestle with the decision to forgive because you have the right to be angry, while the offender does not have the right to kindness. Making the decision to forgive means letting go of these resentments (*which you have every right to hold*) so you can heal.

A lot of people hang on to unforgiveness because they are afraid that forgiving means letting the offender back into their lives, which could cause more harm. This is not so, **forgiving means you are setting yourself free,** and keeping healthy boundaries with the offender, for you this might mean never seeing the person again to keep yourself safe.

REFLECTION

Do you want to keep the resentment, pain and unforgiveness?

Are you willing to let it go?

What are the pros and cons of deciding to forgive the person who wronged you?

Pros:

Cons:

Describe how things might be different if you decide to forgive.

You'll never know how strong your heart is until you learn to forgive who broke it.

OBSERVE

During the process of **letting go** you may start to observe and understand the offender in a new way, which will open up mixed emotions and possibly even positive feelings toward the offender and yourself. Learning to understand the offender, and to see them as more than their wrongdoing, is an important part of forgiveness. However, **it is vital for you to understand** that this does not mean condoning. You can gain understanding and compassion for another person without believing their actions are acceptable.

Observe the object in your hands from the other person's point of view.
- Does it look the same from his/her view?

- Let's look at it from another angle:

- What was life like for this person as they were growing up?

- May this have impacted their behavior?

- What was life like for this person at the time of the offense?

- What feelings do you currently have toward the offender?

JOURNALING

Journal your thoughts and emotions as you look at each of the above questions?

> One of the most courageous decisions you'll ever make is to finally let go of what is hurting your heart and soul.

Observe the painful object in your hands from the point of view of a bystander, someone with an unbiased view. I like to refer to this as the helicopter view. Someone with an un-obstructive point of view.

JOURNAL YOUR OBSERVATION

During the deepening stage of forgiveness, you may find meaning in the experiences, and recognize ways in which you have grown as a result.

Take some time to breathe deep as you notice the emotions you may be experiencing.

- Who is the hardest person to forgive?

- What is it you want to hold onto?

- Have you held onto the pain for long enough now that it might be safe to let it go?

- What benefit is there in forgiving?

- Could you give understanding to yourself and to the other person? Compassion? Acceptance?

- Can you forgive and release?

- Would you be willing to change the belief that you are deserving of the pain to a belief that you are worthy of being loved, protected and cherished?

How willing are you to let go and release, in order to gain the freedom that forgiveness brings?

Release all the pain
All the bitterness
Release the person - let him/her go
Set them free

By setting them free you are setting yourself free.

Say to him/her "I forgive you for not being the way I wanted and needed you to be. I set you free. I set the experience of pain free"

Observe the object in your hand. Has it changed shape or color?

Decide - do you want to let it go completely?

When you feel ready, say the following statements out loud to yourself.

"I forgive _____ and set you free, I forgive myself and set myself free. "I am forgiven, and I am free"

For an audio version of a Forgiveness Journey, copy the following link into your browser.

https://youtu.be/mFnwKLZVaR0

REFLECTION

Consider how forgiveness has affected your emotional health, behavioral changes that resulted from the injustice, and time/energy spent thinking about the offender.

Describe how you have grown because of the pain you endured and your efforts to forgive.

How has your worldview changed?

Are you stronger than you were before deciding to forgive?

What has changed for you during the forgiveness process?

Forgiving is not easy and many times it is a journey that **we need to choose to repeat over and over again** until it does not hold the same bitterness, resentment or fear.

You took a courageous and painful journey today. A journey that is **vital to your freedom and growth.** Unforgiveness is relentless in holding us in a stuck pattern of believing we are victims and not worthy of more in life.

You are worthy and deserving of a life full of joy and freedom.

SELFCARE

Rest - you have been on a journey, and it is time to rest. This may be a hot bath or a stroll in the park or forest. Take time to sit and just breathe, noticing each breath you take, as a gift of life.

HOMEWORK

Write a letter of forgiveness to the person that caused you pain. Tell them about the pain, forgiving them, and that you are no longer holding him/her hostage in your mind/ heart anymore. There's power in the act of writing the words. You may choose to give the letter, or you may choose to keep it for a reminder to yourself of the process you walked through

We think that forgiveness is weakness, but it's absolutely not; it takes a very strong person to forgive. T. D. Jakes

Forgiveness does not change the past, but it does enlarge the future.
– Paul Boose

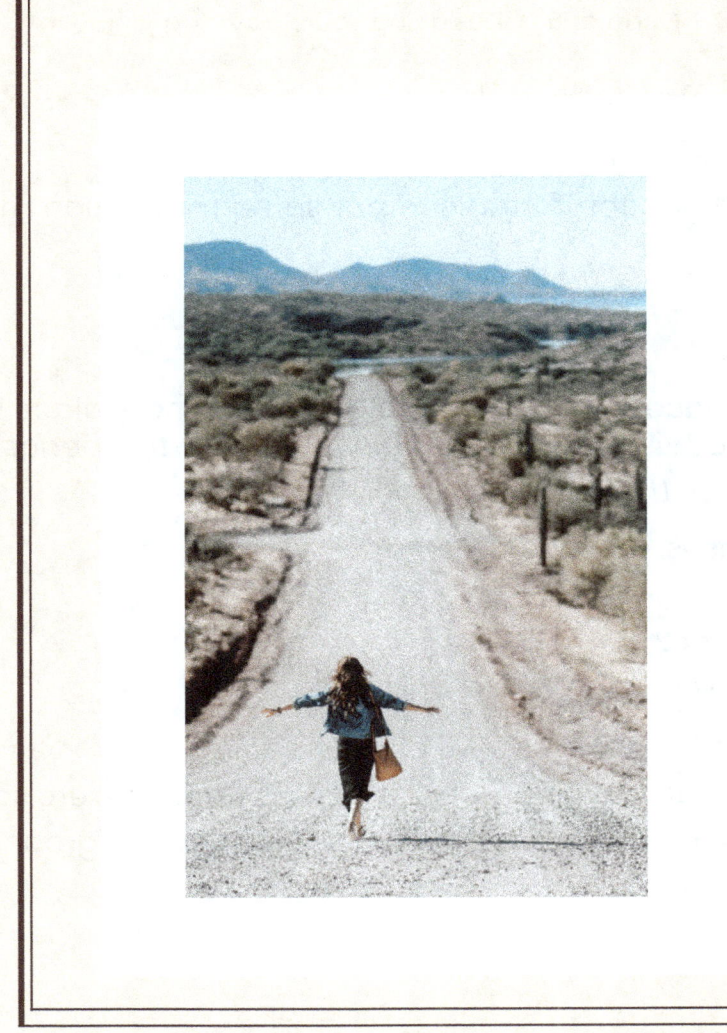

CHAPTER SIX

designing your road map

GROUNDING EXERCISE

Find a space to relax and get comfortable - put some meditation music on to still your heart, mind and soul.

- Pause
- Close your eyes
- Picture a peaceful place, either in real life or an imaginary place in your mind.
- Take five deep breaths *(with each inhale, breath in the peace, with each exhale, picture the stresses of the day leaving your body)*
- Focus on your 4 senses, one at a time
    o What do I feel?
    o What do you see?
    o What do I smell?
    o What do I hear?

Notice how you feel after you have completed this grounding exercise. Notice the muscle tension, has it been released? This breathing exercise is meant to ground you in preparation for today's module.

SONG OF THE DAY

Dare to dream today! Below is a song that has been chosen for you. Be still and let the music and words speak to you.

[A Million Dreams - Charity & Phineas](#)

LET'S BEGIN

If you had unlimited resources and couldn't fail, if you had no fear, what would you set out to do?

If you had all the confidence you want and knew you could not fail in any situation, what would you dare to do?

Setting goals for your life provides direction and is a motivator. Without goals it is difficult to focus and to achieve the dreams you have. It is like a ship at sea without a compass. Or driving through a new country without a roadmap to guide you. **Without a target to aim for, you cannot hit the destination**, so it is important to have goals that are specific, measurable, attainable and action orientated. A goal is an idea or a desired result that you have for your life, a destination you would like to reach.

> *"A dream is your creative vision for your life in the future. A goal is what specifically you intend to happen. Dreams and goals should be just out of your present reach but not out of sight. Dreams and goals are coming attractions in your life" - Joseph Campbell*

What are some of your dreams for your life?

What if for this one day only, anything you dream will come out good - there is no way you can fail. What would you dare to dream if this were true?

It can feel overwhelming to begin with or you may have ideas but feel overwhelmed with attaining them.

LIFE INVENTORY

The LADDER of life is a first step to defining changes you want to make in your life and start setting goals. You completed a life inventory in the Introduction of this course to raise your awareness and to reflect on where you are at. **This** ladder is intended for you to examine close up where you are and where you want to be. Without knowing where you desire to be, you will be like a ship at sea with no rudder, tossed to and fro in the wind. Having a direction to work towards **is the light guiding you.**

Label the steps of the ladder with the categories that are most significant to you.

- Family
- Personal growth
- Self-care
- Exercise/fitness
- Love/Romance
- Friendship

- Finance / Money
- Career/Business
- Health
- Community
- Spirituality
- Housing

The bottom of life represents 0% satisfaction and fulfillment in this area of your life and the top of the ladder represents 100% satisfied and fulfilled. Spend some time putting thought and reflection into this process to create the most accurate picture of your life balance and satisfaction. After you place all of your categories, sit back and reflect on the inventory before you. Are there changes you would like to see in the categories? Are you up the ladder far enough to create a sense of accomplishment and well-being?

Chapter 6 | Designing Your Road Map

Picture the ladder as if it was placed in position, leaning against a cloud marked "goals / dreams". As you look at how far up you have climbed in each category, does the category help you reach your goals and dreams? Or is it hindering your climb? What areas would you like to make changes to in order to create more balance and fulfillment in your life? This exercise can feel discouraging when you are not experiencing fullness and balance, but to be very clear, this is not meant for you to beat yourself up but rather to bring awareness, hope and clarity.

What we do not know, we cannot change.

Defining the changes that you want to make; your goals and destination is something that takes thought and time. But without action steps the goal will remain a dream. It takes beginning with the end in mind and a clear understanding of your destination and where you're going so that you have your compass pointed in the right direction at all times. A focus point to aim for.

Tony Robbins expresses it this way:

"You can't have a plan for your day, until you have a plan for your life."

A lot of people dream and plan with limitations of our own belief systems. What if you dared to dream and think with the potential of a lifetime?

What if for a moment you let your imagination go and visualized a life without limitations and rather looked at the potential that lies within you. The greatness that you have been unlocking for the past few weeks that is begging to be let free.

What if you dared to dream in terms of your potential instead of your current capabilities and the limited belief you have about your circumstances. How would it change your dream and how you perceive your capabilities?

REFLECTION

"Miracle Question" - The following question is a thought-provoking question. Take some time to let yourself explore your dreams and what lies within you.

Imagine that tonight as you sleep a miracle occurs in your life. A magical momentous happening that has completely solved your problems and rippled out to cover and infinitely improve all areas of your life. Your life is exactly like you want it to be. Your career, relationships, where you live.

Think for a moment and tell me how is life different when you wake up and go about your day? What's the first thing you'll notice as you wake up in the morning?

(Used in solution focused therapy created by Insoo Kim Berg & Steven de Shazer)

Describe your day/life in detail.

Chapter 6 | Designing Your Road Map

Now that you have the creativity and vision flowing....

Take 10 minutes to do a brain dump of all of your dreams, goals, aspirations, things you would like to do and achieve, experiences that you would like to have.

What do you really want to do with your life? What would you like to accomplish with your life?

What would you regret not doing if you suddenly found you had a limited amount of time left on the earth?

Hold nothing back, big and small, there is no wrong answer. Write as fast as you can and give yourself permission to dream big.

Brain Dump:

TIMELINE

Create a timeline. *(I found the simplest way of doing this and a good visualization was to tape paper to a wall in a room)*

Begin with the big picture - take the words from the brain dump list, that you want to accomplish in 10 years, another paper labeled 5 years, 4 years and so on until you reach 1 year. This can be career, finances, business, relationships, travel, education, ect. When you reach 1 year, break it down into months until you reach 1 month from today's date.

Be realistic with your times, make them achievable timelines so as not to lose momentum.

Take a step back and reflect on your work. How does it feel to see your dreams as a road map in front of you? It may be overwhelming, hopeful, invigorating.

Is there anything you want to add or take away?

Review your work and break this into smaller steps.

What action steps do you need to take in order to reach each goal?

What action steps do you need to take this week to reach your goal for 1 month from now?

Write these action steps on a schedule so that you have definite dates on which to do things.

Your action steps will be what moves you forward and make that goal a reality. Make them simple, have an accountability partner, tackle them in order of importance.

Take your top 5 goals and write a description for each goal explaining why it is important for you to reach this goal. Why it excites you.

    1.

    2.

    3.

    4.

    5.

Say the goal out loud to yourself, share it with a trusted friend. Speaking it out loud creates a reality and a determination. Let it sink in.

At the end of each month/ year, review what you have completed, mark things off the checklists for each step taken and goal achieved. Write up a schedule with the action points you need for the next year.

Celebrate each goal that you reach. It is important to acknowledge your achievements. Be proud of yourself for the accomplishments.

Your goals can transform your life in ways that help you unlock the extraordinary in you!

Here's a question to ponder - Is it more painful to keep all your hopes, dreams, goals, desires locked up inside of you or get them out there into the world, pursue them, and possibly fail but know you gave it everything and experienced the journey?

Keep your heart open. Be observant when you are at your happiest, healthiest, and most energized. Life has a way of telling you when you need to step into another goal, or that a goal no longer fits for who you are.

Review what limitations or obstacles might come in your way of achieving your destination?

What do you need to put into place to remove anI am excited for you as you take these essential and significant steps towards walking more fully in your greatness. d/or support you through these obstacles?

Imagine you are 80 years old and looking back at your life, which dream from your list would cause the greatest regret if you had NOT pursued it? What is the cost of not pursuing it? What Is the benefit? How will your life look different if you pursue and accomplish your dream? How will it look if you do not?

Reaching Your goals is not an easy journey. **It takes perseverance, dedication, a lot of courage and stepping outside your comfort zone.** But the more you practice using these tools for the journey, the stronger you become. Until one day it is more uncomfortable to NOT step into the courage and move forward than it is to stay in the comfort zone and not achieve your goals.

Goals big and small can be the stepping-stones to a fulfilled, passionate life that you get to create.

> *In the end, the overriding factor is whether or not you realize your dreams are going to be you. Not the world. YOU. – Russel Simmons*

You are going to be the moving force behind the achievement of your dreams. You will be the one to say stop or go.

Take this little mantra that I learnt years ago at a conference to remind you on days when it feels hard:

> *If I always do what I have always done, I will always get what I have always gotten.*

Be – committed to
Do – what it takes to
Have – what you want

I am excited for you as you take these essential and significant steps towards walking more fully in your greatness and into the man / woman that you are designed and created to be..

SELF-CARE

Invite a trusted friend to go for a coffee, share your dreams and goals with each other. Take time to laugh and enjoy friendship. Part of self-care is taking care of your relationships and part of conquering your goals is sharing them with a trusted friend. This sharing makes the dream and goal become more of a reawltiy.

HOMEWORK

Review your goals every day for the next month. **Read it, say it**.
Example - "when I am a teacher" "when I go to Greece"

Make your goals as your opening screen on your phone and/or computer as a reminder of your goal. Of why you get up early each morning and persevere when you feel like giving up.

In the next segment we will explore your purpose and why. This adds a whole new dynamic to staying in the 'go zone' for goals.

"Live the Life of Your Dreams: Be brave enough to live the life of your dreams

according to your vision and purpose instead of the expectations and opinions of others." - Roy T. Bennett

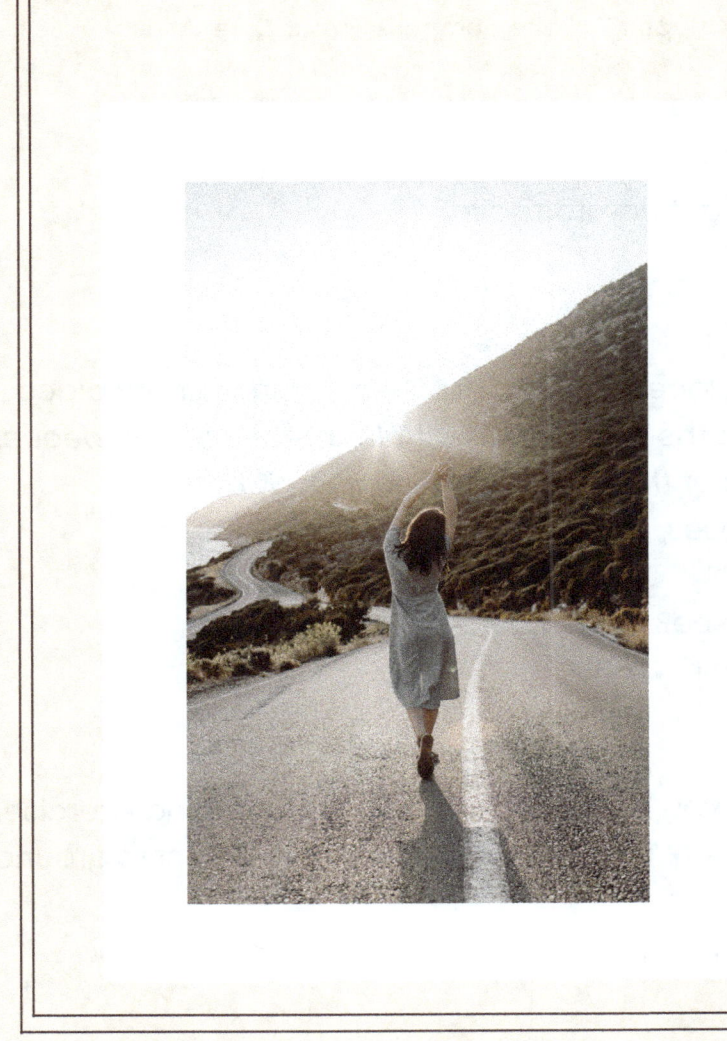

CHAPTER SEVEN
life compass
your core values

GROUNDING EXERCISE

Find a space to relax and get comfortable:

- Pause
- Close your eyes
- Picture a peaceful place, either in real life or an imaginary place in your mind.
- Take five deep breaths *(with each inhale, breath in the peace, with each exhale, picture the stresses of the day leaving your body)*
- Focus on your 4 senses, one at a time
    - What do I feel?
    - What do you see?
    - What do I smell?
    - What do I hear?

Notice how you feel after you have completed this grounding exercise. Notice the muscle tension, has it been released? This breathing exercise is meant to ground you in preparation for today's module.

SONG OF THE DAY

The most beautiful gift you can give yourself and the world around you is by being the best version of yourself! Below is a song that has been chosen for you. Be still and let the music and words speak to you.

[Dare to Be by Tenille](#)

LET'S BEGIN

You have done some really difficult and soul-searching work. **You can be incredibly proud of yourself.** Do a check in with yourself and tune in to how you are feeling with the work you have done. You might be feeling lighter, exhausted, worn thin, hopeful, courageous. There is no wrong feeling, just tune in and sense where you are at.

In this segment you are going to look at what is important to you in life. I call these foundational values - Your life compass.

What are foundational values and why are they important?

I like how John C Maxwell states it:

"Your core values are the deeply held beliefs that authentically describe your soul."

Your foundational values are a personal code for guiding your choices, actions, behaviors and responses. They are what guides your decisions in your personal life, relationships, business, career, your family life, your choices and behaviors. They are your life compass.

Discovering your personal foundational values will provide you with greater understanding and awareness of who you are and why you make the decisions you make, doing the things you do, helping you maximize your potential as a person.

I also like to look at foundational values as a compass in life that guides us. When you do not operate in your values and honor them, you will have difficulty in achieving your fullest potential. Life is automatically in more of an alignment and flow when we let our foundational values be a compass.

"Peace of mind comes when your life is in harmony with true principles and values and in no other way." Stephen Covey

It can also be easy to live by values someone else has put on us if we are not in tune to our values and daily checking in on our personal values compass.

Chapter 7 | Life Compass – Your Core Values

Most of us don't know our values. We don't understand what's most important to us. Rather, we put our focus and beliefs on what our society, culture, family of origin media tell us.

Living life without a sense of our foundational values is like walking into a store and buying a pair of jeans with our eyes closed. We are there but not seeing what we are purchasing, likely we will purchase something that does not fit and makes us feel uncomfortable and dissatisfied. So, it is with our values. Living outside of our foundational values can leave us feeling frustrated and discontent with our lives and circumstances that happen.

Every situation in life is controlled by your beliefs and by your values.

Values are a strong foundation from which we base our thinking, choices, behaviors, actions and even, conversation from. They tell a story about who we are, what we believe in and why we are the way we are. They tell a story of the **unique character and nature of you.**

When you have a solid sense of yourself and live from your core values, **you are living from the essence of who you are, of who you were created to be. Your unique beautiful self.**

When you honor your personal foundational values on a consistent basis, you experience fulfillment, happiness and a sense of purpose and meaning in life

What you value is where you place your time and attention, it is what you focus on. Are you focusing on what is most important to you?

When you align with your values, and what you desire in life, you will experience a sense of fulfillment and accomplish your goals with a greater sense of ease, alternatively, when your values are not in alignment with your vision and purpose for your life there will be an unrest and an enormous amount of grit, push and effort. By acknowledging and taking responsibility for the life that you have created, you are taking the first step to aligning your values. You will look at what is MOST important to you and choose beliefs and values according to your vision.

Your values will be a light on the path to your vision. **Your compass. They will light up in your heart knowing that you are on the right path.** They will help you to evaluate decisions and choices that are before you. Your values will inspire you to make decisions that create a sense of empowerment within you. **They are your 'decision making blueprint'.**

Knowing your foundational values will help you to set boundaries and to say 'yes' to the things that are in alignment with those values and to say 'no' to the things that are not aligning.

Stephen Covey expresses it this way:

"Begin each day with the blueprint of my deepest values FIRMLY in mind then when challenges come, make decisions BASED on those values."

Your personal values are an **essential part of who you are, and who you want to be.** Exploring and discovering your core values is a challenging, insightful and important exercise.

DIGGING DEEPER – *Reflect and Journal*

Identify a time that you were the happiest in your life.

Identify a time that was most meaningful to you.

What was meaningful about this occasion?

What were you doing?

Which values were you honoring?

Identify a time when you felt the proudest?

What were you doing?

What factors contributed to the proud moment?

What values were you honoring in this moment?

Consider times that you felt the most fulfilled and content.

What factors contributed to the feelings of fulfillment and contentment?

How did this experience give your life meaning?

What values were you honoring in this experience?

Now let's explore the opposite: identify a time that you felt angry, upset or frustrated. What was happening for you in this moment?

What values were being suppressed or opposed at this moment?

VALUES DISCOVERY

What are your personal foundational values? Spend some time in reflection - What insight did you gain from the questions above? What is most important to you? What you cannot live without in your life; spiritually physical emotional, relational, What makes you feel like you are aligned and happy - you and what you are doing is right with the world in this moment?

A quick Internet search for 'core or personal values' may lead you to tools to assist you in refining this discovery of your foundational values.

Journal your insights and reflections on this page. Define your foundational values - the bottom line of what you cannot live without in your life. The essence of you!
Example: compassion, drive, fun, harmony

List your top 6 can't live without foundational values below in order of importance to alignment in your life. What 6 foundational values are my life compass and essential to my life?

1. _____

2. _____

3. _____

4. _____

5. _____

6. _____

REFLECTION

Let's take a closer look at these 5 core values. Do your values align with the purpose for your life?

Do you feel your values are in the order of importance to you?
(list them in order of importance)

1. _____

2. _____

3. _____

4. _____

5. _____

6. _____

Which values are essential to supporting 'who you are'?

Which values represent your behaviors and actions - your primary way of being?

Are these values personal to you?

Do these values resonate and give you a sense of peace and belonging?

Do these values feel consistent with who you are OR do they represent a value that was placed on you by someone else? Example. A parent, society, authority figure

What's your level of satisfaction of how each value is honored in your life? Score each of your top 6 foundational values below.

not honored	somewhat honored	fully honored

0_____5_____10

This exercise brings awareness to how each value is expressed in your day-to-day life. If you scored below a 7, ask yourself what changes do you need to make in order to more fully honor this particular value?

When was a time you fully embraced your most important values?

How have I honored my values and how did I feel?

What are some ways I can lean more fully into my values?

Did I risk in honor of holding true to my values? What were you risking?

"As you live your values, your sense of identity, integrity, control, and inner-directedness will infuse you with both exhilaration and peace. You will define yourself from within, rather than by people's opinions or by comparisons to others." Stephen Covey

Do a check-in with your personal foundational values again:

Do you feel a difference in your level of fulfillment and contentment in life as you **imagine** living in your foundational values and begin to live in your foundational values.

At this moment, how would you fill in the following blank using one word:

"At my core I am _____". *(List value)*

As you learn to lean into your foundational values, you will begin to let the values define your decision making and the direction the compass points for all your life choices. As opportunities are presented you can ask yourself. "Does this opportunity align with what I believe in?"

Most important is this next question, "Does this align with the purpose for my life?"

When you feel restlessness, unease, or discontent, ask yourself 'Which value am I not honoring at this moment?

Let your foundational values be a compass for your life. Make it a habit to check-in daily with your life compass. Your values will impact your career, relationship, family, and personal decisions.

By staying in tune to your core values you will be tapping in daily to the greatness that lies within you.

SELF-CARE
Schedule self-care time in your calendar like you would schedule in an important appointment. Plan time for some fun that aligns with your values.

HOMEWORK
Write your values on a paper, sticky note or your phone's home screen. Somewhere that you can see it every day. Take 5 minutes each day to read them and reflect on how you are honoring your values that day.

"The more you know who you are, and what you want, the less you let things upset you." Stephanie Perkins

We don't have to be perfect, just engaged and committed to aligning values with actions. -Brené Brown

Chapter 7 | Life Compass – Your Core Values

CHAPTER EIGHT
you shine: strengths

GROUNDING EXERCISE

Find a space to relax and get comfortable - put some relaxation / meditation music on as you quiet your mind and prepare your heart for todays chapter.
- Pause
- Close your eyes
- Picture a peaceful place, either in real life or an imaginary place in your mind.
- Take five deep breaths *(with each inhale, breath in the peace, with each exhale, picture the stresses of the day leaving your body)*
- Focus on your 4 senses, one at a time
    o What do I feel?
    o What do you see?
    o What do I smell?
    o What do I hear?

Notice how you feel after you have completed this grounding exercise. Notice the muscle tension, has it been released? This breathing exercise is meant to ground you in preparation for today's module.

SONG OF THE DAY

You are a gift to the world around you - Below is a song that has been chosen for you. Be still and let the music and words speak to you.

The Gift You Are - John Denver

LET'S BEGIN

If someone asked you today what are your gifts and strengths? How would you respond? And how quickly can you respond if you are asked what your weaknesses are? We are often quick to focus on our weaknesses and are unsure about our gifting and strengths.

In this segment we are going to explore what your gifts and strengths are and how knowing your strengths, that are a part of your unique personality style can greatly benefit your life.

One of the most powerful tools in life is to know what your gifts and strengths are and accept the **incredible gift they are to you and the incredible gift YOU are to the world around you.** When you hide your strengths and do not use them, you are missing out, and so are others. You are designed and created uniquely with a unique set of gifts and strengths for a reason and when you do not show up with those strengths... the world misses out.

WHAT IS A GIFT OR STRENGTH?

Strengths are personal abilities that come naturally to you. Abilities that you excel at. I like to call these gifts. **A gift is something you are born with and comes naturally to you.**

Those who use their natural strengths and gifts achieve the most in life as they are operating out of a natural flow

So, it is important to be self - aware. Knowing yourself, what your strengths and weaknesses are can help you know where you need to focus on improvement and where you can focus for greater results.

We do not usually enjoy looking at our flaws, but so often tend to do so, letting the inner judge highlight when we are not at our best. It is important to take an objective look at yourself to identify what your strengths and weaknesses are so you can **more fully walk in your strengths and take a constructive approach to your weaknesses.** When you can identify your weaknesses, you can learn to consciously develop these areas or outsource them where possible.

You might ask... What Is the difference between a strength and a core value? Strengths are a part of the character that is a natural part of a person which, when you are using your strengths it brings a sense of authenticity, and a feeling of excitement while displaying them. A value is like a life compass, bringing direction into your one amazing life.

Why is it so important to know your best gifts and strengths?

Individuals that know their strengths are more confident, self-accepting and have a higher self-esteem. They tend to be happier and more satisfied with life, experiencing less stress and knowing how to utilize their strengths to assist them through stressful situations. Knowing your gifts and strengths will instill feelings of authenticity and a more positive mindset. **When you know your gifts and strengths your choices and behaviors will be more in tune with what you do best and excel in.**

Focusing on what you do well instead of on your flaws will have a real positive impact on your lifestyle and sense of well-being by fully developing and applying your strengths. When you function in your gifts and strengths you will feel natural at using your abilities and further developing them.

A sense of positive energy comes along with using gifts and strengths and will flow together with your core values and satisfies an inner need to live in a place of using your best gifts and to continue to apply them to your daily life

Knowing and focusing on your gifts and strengths will extend the vision you have of yourself and of what you are capable of doing with this precious life you are given.

Some of your gifts and strengths you will recognize in yourself already, while others will be more subtle and difficult to identify.

MINING FOR GOLD

You are uniquely you, designed and created with a special set of strengths, traits and gifts. We often do not recognize these qualities in ourselves until we dig for them, examining and looking at our behaviors and actions, acknowledging what we excel at.

Answering the following questions is mining for the strengths that you may not have seen in yourself.

Chapter 8 | You Shine - Strengths

Answer the following questions to mine for the gifts and strengths that you may not have seen in yourself. **Take some time to list your talents, skills, characteristics, behaviors, and areas of greatest knowledge.** It may feel difficult and like self-bragging but give yourself permission to acknowledge where you shine.

What activities were you naturally drawn to as a child?

What is easy and effortless for you to do today? What comes naturally?

What do you do especially well?

What is enjoyable and fun for you to do?

What are your greatest successes? Why?

What are your strongest character traits?

What energizes you?

What activity gives you a sense of fulfillment and purpose?

What makes you unique?

What activities or tasks do you gravitate to and do effortlessly?

When you have time to do something you truly enjoy, what are you doing?

When you find yourself in the "zone or flow" what are you doing?

What activities do you get completely absorbed in?

What qualities do you have that you could not do life without?

What is the most enjoyable job/career you have had?

What was it about this job/career that you enjoyed the most?

What would your closest friend say are your gifts /strengths?

Gifts and strengths you use to help others and create joy for another?

WHAT ARE YOUR GIFTS AND STRENGTHS?

Brain dump - Create an exhaustive list of the gifts and strengths that have naturally been placed inside you - from the questions above and what you instinctively know are apart of who you are.

List your top 5 gifts and strengths.

1. _____
2. _____
3. _____
4. _____
5. _____

REFLECTION

Which gifts and strengths are most important with accomplishing your **life goals**? *(refer back to module 6)*

What gifts and strengths will best help you to become the person you want to be?

Reflect on compliments you have been given! What do others see in you that create the compliment?

Do these compliments align with your strengths?

What strengths will help me to become the person I am created to be?

JOURNAL

Be still and reflect on the gifts and strengths you have discovered - have you missed any? How do you feel as you acknowledge these gifts and strengths?

IDENTIFYING WEAKNESSES

Now that you have listed your strengths, let's take a brief moment to examine weaknesses that you have. Everyone has weaknesses and it is important to know both, what your strengths and your weaknesses are so that you can **learn to manage them.**

When you know your weaknesses, **you can say 'yes' to the things that energize you and bring a sense of purpose to your life and 'no' to the activities that don't serve your greater purpose and life goals,** or learn how to 'staff' your weaknesses.

What are the weaknesses that you are aware of?

What do you tend to avoid?

What causes you to 'give up' when tackling a project?

What is an energy drainer for you?

What would you call your blind-spot? (*An area you struggle to understand or see the importance of*)

What holds you back from moving forward? What is your roadblock?

While awareness of weaknesses is good it is important for you to keep your focus on your strengths as **'what you focus on is the direction you go. Be aware** of what your blind spots are and **focus on the strengths and gifting you have.**

GIFTS / STRENGTHS

As you step more fully into your 'you', you will choose which behaviors and activities you wish to eliminate, strengthen or change in order to walk more fully in your unique and deeper purpose.

A gift and strength will give you energy when you are actively using them. You will feel motivated with a sense of enjoyment and fulfillment. It will feel more natural to you and a part of who you are.

There may be strengths that you have that have been suppressed in life and may need some coaxing to flourish. It doesn't mean this is not a strength, it just may take some **'stepping out of your comfort zone.**

Your gifts and strengths are what come naturally to you. When you discover your greatest strengths, you learn to use them to handle stress and challenges, you can improve your life and thrive in all areas as you become happier, and develop healthy relationships with those who matter most to you.

I love and highly value how Gallup describes Strengths.

> "Excellence, not average, is your measure. Taking something from below average to slightly above average takes a great deal of effort and in your opinion is not very rewarding. Transforming something strong into something superb takes just as much effort but is much more thrilling. Strengths, whether yours or someone else's, fascinate you. Like a diver after pearls, you search them out, watching for the telltale signs of strength. A glimpse of untutored excellence, rapid learning, a skill mastered without recourse to steps — all these are clues that a strength may be in play. And having found a strength, you feel compelled to nurture it, refine it, and stretch it toward excellence. You polish the pearl until it shines. This natural sorting of strengths means that others see you as discriminating. You choose to spend time with people who appreciate your particular strengths. Likewise, you are attracted to others who seem to have found and cultivated their own strengths. You tend to avoid those who want to fix you and make you well rounded. You don't want to spend your life

bemoaning what you lack. Rather, you want to capitalize on the gifts with which you are blessed. It's more fun. It's more productive. And, counterintuitively, it is more demanding." (www.gallup.com/cliftonstrengths)

You will strengthen your strength muscles by using them.

Be adventurous and step outside your comfort zone. Often. Growth happens outside the comfort zone and your gifts and strengths will shine when you use them.

Another quick Internet search for strengths may lead you to tools to assist you in refining this discovery of your gifts and strengths.

JOURNAL

Reflect on the insights have you gained from this module and the exercises? Journal the insights you have gained. Were you surprised by the gifts and strengths that you discovered? Did you gain a greater clarity for why you do some of the things you do? Maybe a deeper understanding of the purpose over your life?

SELFCARE

Step outside your comfort zone today. Find one activity that stretches you, yes this is part of self-care.

Put on your favorite music and dance for 5 minutes or more. Dance with your partner, your friends, your children, or dance solo. Just dance. Feel the energy!

HOMEWORK

Ask ten people who know you well to write down strengths, gifts and qualities they see in you when they have witnessed you at your best. You might ask "how do you experience me? Ask individuals that come from diverse backgrounds including friends, mentors, family, colleagues, managers.

Identify patterns among the feedback you receive. Which strengths do you see repeated? Create a self-portrait, outlining the strengths you discovered in yourself, and the strengths as perceived by the sources above who know you and have seen you at your best. **Put your strengths to work and shine**

"She remembered who she was and the game changed." - Lalah Delia

"Authenticity is the daily practice of letting go of who we think we're supposed to be and embracing who we are." Brene Brown

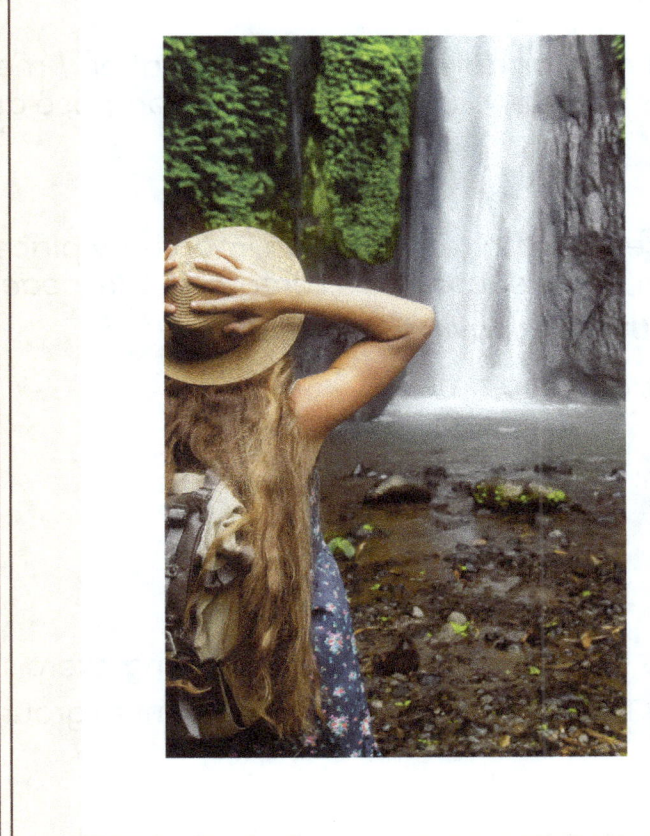

CHAPTER NINE

mining deeper for gold

GROUNDING EXERCISE

Find a space to relax and get comfortable - put some relaxation / mediation music on to prepare your heart for todays chapter as you explore your purpose and why.

- Pause
- Close your eyes
- Picture a peaceful place, either in real life or an imaginary place in your mind.
- Take five deep breaths *(with each inhale, breath in the peace, with each exhale, picture the stresses of the day leaving your body)*
- Focus on your 4 senses, one at a time
    o What do I feel?
    o What do you see?
    o What do I smell?
    o What do I hear?

Notice how you feel after you have completed this grounding exercise. Notice the muscle tension, has it been released? This breathing exercise is meant to ground you in preparation for today's module.

SONG OF THE DAY

Finding why you were put here and how you can make an impact and difference is not easy, but it is exciting. Below is a song that has been chosen for you. Be still and let the music and words speak to you.

Are you Ready (on your own) Distant Cousins
Brave - Sara Bareilles

LET'S BEGIN

How does one define 'life purpose"? There comes a defining moment in life, when you feel that what you're doing aligns with your head and your heart, and with the giftings, strengths, values and talents you have, while you are making a difference and filling a need in the world around you.

I like this quote by John Maxwell:

> "Your calling is your purpose with a divine touch."

When you have a sense of your life purpose and know your 'WHY', you are doing what you love to do. You no longer just go through the motions but are **being intentional with your day-to-day actions and decisions.**

There comes a time in most of our lives, where we ask a far-reaching question. 'What am I on this earth for?" We may spend months and years searching for the answer to this question and feel frustrated if we do not know 'now' what purpose we have.

You may feel that there is no purpose for your life, but look closely and get curious! Spend intentional time daring to dream big!

Your life purpose becomes a motivating influence - while it guides your life decisions, actions and behaviors, it also helps to shape your goals and gives you a sense of direction. **It creates a desire for every day to be more meaningful and to have a greater impact on the world around you**, filling a void in your life and a void or need in the world.

You may even wonder if you have a purpose and feel like you don't have a place on this earth. I am here to tell you; you do have a purpose and a reason for being. You are valued and desperately needed, someone somewhere needs You, they need you and your story to encourage them to keep going. They need you to be the difference for them. You have a purpose, and the exciting part is, if you are unsure what it is, you get to go on a journey to discover what that is for you.

Within each of us there lies an innate desire to make a difference. As a young child and teen years, especially as we neared the end of high school years, there was always a question that carried a certain mystery in it. 'What do you want to be when you grow up?' as we become adults that question often still has an evasive ring to it. Who do I want to be? How can I make a difference or an impact?

Oft times this is overwhelming to understand and figure out and we wish someone would just stand behind us, put a hand on our shoulder and another pointing the way ahead saying ' go this way to make a difference, this is the way, go and do it, this is your purpose."

It is not quite that easy... figuring out your life purpose is something only you can explore and find the answer to.

The answer lies within you. It is like mining for gold, the deeper you dig into discovering more about yourself the more you will discover the passions that are waiting to be exposed.

It is often a process of life experiences that slowly brings to light the purpose burning in your heart. Life experiences, the good, the bad and the ugly, peel back the layer and prepare you for that greater purpose. It is like the refining fire, or the potter and the clay, molding you through life experiences until the shaping has created passion and desires with in you.

While you are being shaped and molded, be intentional to be the best version of who you were created and designed to be.

When you live with gratitude and intention you are living a life on purpose. To lead a life on purpose, follow the passions of your heart. Follow what makes your heart sing and feel full!

There is not just one purpose for you, there may be multiple passions that you have that all make up your **uniquely designed purpose and meaning for life.**

I am a mom. That is a life purpose for me. To be the best mom I can be and to raise my young men into men of honor. I also have another passion I call a purpose and that is helping you to see the beauty and uniqueness that makes you the **spectacular and amazing person that you are**. Another purpose of mine is to make a difference in the lives of women across the globe, inspiring and motivating to be each woman to be the best version of herself

Purpose in life is to love life fully by putting yourself completely into showing up for yourself and stepping boldly into what you are passionate about and what excites you.

This will mean at times stepping into the unknown with shaky legs and doing what is before you regardless of how inadequate you feel for the job at hand. **It is showing up and letting yourself be seen where you are called to be seen.**

The feeling that something is missing in your life can be a gift as it is inviting you to explore and discover what brings you a sense of fulfillment and passion. When you don't feel connected in life, it is an opportunity for self-discovery and digging deeper into more of an awareness of what really matters to you and what your heart desires.

Darlene Brock expresses it this way -

"Within us is everything we need, to become who we are to become, it just needs to be mined and nurtured and developed, it takes grit to discover it and grace to fail in the process."

Oftentimes, we look at our life story and wonder what good can come from it, however, **our greatest purpose in life may come directly from the messiness of the story**. When you can take your mess and turn it into a message that impacts someone's life you may be offering the greatest hope, encouragement and inspiration to change a life.

Your messy may be the catalyst for someone else's victory or healing.

Messes, accomplishments, and goals, big and small, can be the stepping-stones to a fulfilled, passionate life that you get to create.

By uncovering your gifts, talents, and passions **you can light the world up by showing up and being the best version of who you were created to be.**

Your heart is going to be the guidepost for accessing your passions and purposes in life When you are inspired, connected, and feel like your heart is full you will be motivated to explore and to gain valuable insight into what brings you the most joy and happiness

MINING DEEPER FOR GOLD

Let's begin exploring some aspects of your life that you may deem as unimportant but are insightful to your life purpose. Connect the dots from your childhood, through your teen years and into adulthood. How have you always made a positive difference in people's lives?

What did you love to do as a child? What did you excel at? What made you feel proud, accomplished, and happy?

What makes you feel that way now?

Describe a time in your life – a specific experience – where you felt you were fully alive, as if everything you had gone through in life had prepared you for this defining moment and like you were doing what you were born to do?

What do you excel at in life as an adult?

What matters most in life to you?

What solution would you like to bring to the world?

What makes your heart expand and feel determined?

What would you do if you knew you couldn't fail?

What would you do even if nobody paid you to do it?

What makes you come alive?

What activities would bring you more joy and meaning?

What makes you cry, or makes you angry?

If it were not for money, time, and personal responsibilities what would you really love to do with your life?

If you were free to do whatever you wanted, you had nothing stopping you such as time or money, what would you begin doing tomorrow morning?

Do you see a pattern emerging from your answers to the questions? Do you feel a tug at your heartstrings in a specific direction? Explain

Your actions help to define you and the purpose you have in life. Intentionally taking action is an essential step towards becoming more grounded in who you are meant to be. At the end of life, what do you want to be remembered for?

If you were to write an obituary for yourself, what would you want it to say? What legacy do you want to leave behind/ how will the world be a better place because you lived?

Write a paragraph, as if you were writing your obituary, what do you want to be remembered for?

Picture yourself again at your 90th birthday party? Who is there with you celebrating this amazing life you have lived? What accomplishments are you celebrated for? What milestones are remembered and celebrated? Create a picture in your mind's eye of you. Did you fulfill your goals? Did you take action and live a fulfilled life, one full of action? Are you someone that lived life to the fullest, no questions asked, who relentlessly pursued every opportunity that came your way with confidence, and a zest and zeal for life? Can you say you lived without regrets of having pursued your hearts desires and made a lasting impact on the people around you?

Journal the above picture - Your 90th birthday celebration

YOUR PURPOSE

The key to uncovering your life purpose is to start living as if you have already reached the goal and are living out of a place of purpose.

It takes dedication, perseverance, and hard work to achieve the fulfilling life of living in your purpose. It does not happen overnight. **Honoring what you love to do** and moving away from what exhausts and drains you. **It takes stepping outside of your comfort zone over and over again**.

It takes making changes and taking charge of your life. Remember the feeling of being at your 90th birthday party and celebrating You and all your accomplishments over the last 9 decades. Let that feeling fuel your drive to keep going even when it is hard. To **keep discovering the greatness of who you are and what you were placed on this earth for**.

When you allow the positive qualities within you that bring you a sense of meaning, delight and purpose will be amplified and allowed to shine more brightly creating a confidence overflow to those you come in contact with.

YOU are your life on purpose!

Knowing your life purpose and what fulfills you may compel you to take on challenges that will stretch you as much as they inspire you. When you're motivated and empowered by a clear purpose, there is very little that will. hold back from accomplishing what **lights your heart and soul up**

EXPLORE – BOOK TITLE

If you were to write a book of your life story until today. What would the title of your book be?

Spend some time on this question, put some thought into it as it can have a profound effect on how you view your story and the impact it has today.

The title of my life book is_____

DEFINING YOUR WHY

It is the purpose, cause or belief that drives every one of us. Your WHY is the one constant that will guide you toward fulfillment in your work and life.

Knowing what your 'why' is will help you to stay committed to your dreams and goals and will keep you focused on action steps needed to reach a place of fulfillment. It is the reason that drives you to do what you do, the real deepest reason for striving to reach your life purpose.

When you are in a place of discouragement and wondering what is next, your why will be the light that guides you.

Your why is tied to your passions and your purpose, and is reflected in what excites you, what makes you happy, how you can serve the world, and what your strengths and talents are as we explored previously.

REFLECTION

- What makes you excited?
- What energizes you to jump out of bed in the morning?
- What am I naturally good at?
- What do other people ask me to do?
- What makes you happy?
- If money were no object, what would you do?
- What causes a positive ripple effect around me?

Brain dump
Write fast and steady. Write your answers to the above questions and anything else that comes to mind, write non-stop, anything that comes to your mind, this is not a thinking exercise but rather another brain dump.

Chapter 9 | Mining Deeper for Gold – Your Purpose & Why

Do you see a pattern that emerged in the brain dump?

Fill in the following statement - insert your goal and your reason for the goal.

I want to _____

so that _____.

Dig deep here and continue asking WHY? This is important... as you mine down into what really matters to you it will become clearer to you what your why is.

Continue making statements, asking why? after each statement you create until there is no further answer.

> *Example:*
> *I want to make more money so that I can have freedom. Why?*
> *I want freedom so that I can travel and help people. Why?*
> *I want to travel and help people so that they can live fulfilled lives Why?*
> *I want people to live fulfilled lives so that _____ Why?*

You get the idea...Keep mining down until you have no further answers.

As you look at your final sentence, does it feel like a defining statement for you? Does it feel like your why?

Write your purpose and why statement below:

A why statement will be simple, clear, contributing, actionable and expressed in a language that affirms your purpose.

I want to _____
so that _____.

My WHY is –

> "To empower and equip individuals in overcoming obstacles, discovering their God' beauty and who they are, so they can reach their goals and dreams while living uninhibited with boldness." - Ellen Reimer

Write your own purpose and why statement below:

Once you find the "Why "that speaks to your soul, your next question is, "What am I waiting for?"

Ask yourself "what decision can I make right now that will spur me into action and help me to stay committed to living my purpose and why."

When you know your 'why' and live out of a place of 'purpose', **you let your inner light shine to the world around you.** The most beautiful space is when you can live your purpose with a bold authenticity, letting your true self shine.

SELF-CARE

Alone Time - *This is easy for some people and very difficult for others. Being comfortable in your own presence is so important.* Create some space for alone time this week. It may be going to the movies solo, sitting in a coffee shop or an evening at home alone to do what you want. Reflect on the hard work you have done, be proud of you.

Do something that made you happy as a child. Do it unashamedly. When was the last time you felt carefree and deliriously happy? Go do something that makes you feel carefree and giddy with happiness and fun.

HOMEWORK

Write your Why Statement somewhere that you will see it every day. When you feel that you have come up against a wall or feel like giving up, read your 'Why' Statement until you feel the courage to keep pushing forward. Let your 'Why' statement be a call to your soul each day to show up and shine.

I believe we're all put on this planet for a purpose, and we all have a different purpose. -Ellen DeGeneres

"Believe in Your Heart
Believe in your heart that you're meant to live a life full of passion, purpose, magic and miracles." - Roy T. Bennett

CHAPTER TEN

beautiful authentic you

GROUNDING EXERCISE

Find a space to relax and get comfortable - put some relaxation / meditation music on as you relax into this breathing exercise.

- Pause
- Close your eyes
- Picture a peaceful place, either in real life or an imaginary place in your mind.
- Take five deep breaths *(with each inhale, breath in the peace, with each exhale, picture the stresses of the day leaving your body)*
- Focus on your 4 senses, one at a time
    - What do I feel?
    - What do you see?
    - What do I smell?
    - What do I hear?

Notice how you feel after you have completed this grounding exercise. Notice the muscle tension, has it been released? This breathing exercise is meant to ground you in preparation for today's module.

SONG OF THE DAY

My hope for you is that as you look back over the last few weeks, you can see and feel the change in your heart, and you have a new courage and boldness to live your best life and dance while you do it. Below is a song that has been chosen for you. Be still and let the music and words speak to you.

You FIND YOUR WAY (Official Lyric Video FIND MY WAY)
I Hope You Dance - Lee Ann Womack

LET'S BEGIN

Wow. we have spent 9 weeks together. How are you doing? I wish I could sit down in a coffee shop with you and as we drink our lattes, I would love to hear how your experience has been the last 9 weeks. How is life different for you? Do you have a new perspective on your story and who you are as a woman?

Do you have a renewed hope for your future?

Do you have a deeper sense of knowing your value and worth?

"I wish you could see yourself today how other people see you, those that love you for who you are."

The beautiful and courageous human that you are.

Today we are going to wrap up our time together in this lesson plan. I want to give you some takeaways as you move forward in your life.

First and foremost, never forget that you are uniquely and delightfully made for a purpose.

SELF-CARE

Self-care needs to be **an essential part of your life every day**. Not just every now and them, but every day.

Some people have the notion that self-care is some extravagant, expensive and time-consuming task that leaves a hole in the wallet. But I dare to differ with you on that. Self-care **is taking care of you**. Self-care is **being comfortable in your own presence**. It is taking a walk, having an exercise routine. You have only one body and **your body's a vessel to be treasured and looked after**. We cannot just go and buy another body like we do a new car or a new pair of shoes when the old ones wear out.

Self-care is eating healthy and nutritional meals with the odd splurge of ice-cream and chocolate. Everybody craves 'that' snack at some time in their week. Shh. I will tell you mine but don't tell anyone else. Pure peanut butter, pure dark chocolate, melted together. And then I love to dip apple pieces into it. This was passed onto me by a health nutritionist and is a favorite go to when I am craving a healthier dessert.

Having time for friends and family is a part of self-care and keeping a balance between work and social life. Check in with yourself often to see how you are doing here. It is really easy to get so preoccupied with the demands of life that we forget that a selfcare need is connection with your tribe.

Schedule 'you time' into your calendar as if it is an appointment with your client, boss, or dentist.

You are important to show up for you.

Do what you love and what makes your soul sing. Play, take time to be silly, laugh, create opportunity for a good ole' belly laugh with someone you love. Dance, stop and smell the beauty of a flower, jump in puddle, make a paper airplane, maybe your self-care is to buy yourself a bouquet of flowers, it doesn't need to be the most expensive bundle of roses, if you are on a budget maybe the $4 bundle of Gerber daisies or tulips is your bright spot in the day.

GRATITUDE

Take time to delight in the beauty around you. Practice gratefulness, keep a gratitude journal

Look for the little things to be thankful for. Look for the moments of joy and delight. **Let yourself delight in the simple pleasures.**

- my eyes
- the sunshine
- a warm house to live in
- a cozy blanket
- a listening ear
- laughter
- chocolate covered strawberry
- freshly laundered clothes
- a picnic
- the smell of fresh cut grass
- a perfect slice of juicy watermelon

The list goes on and on

A heart of gratitude shifts the mindset and shifts a day.

Chapter 10 | Beautiful Authentic You

COMPARISON
You, **yes fire comparison**. Comparison kills joy, friendships, and kindness. Stop comparing yourself to others. This is part of self-care. Rather **have a curiosity for yourself and what your beautiful self has to offer the world.** There is no one like you and when we compare and try so hard to fit in, you are robbing the world around you of the beauty of YOU. Stop scrolling through social media **and focus on what truly brings you joy**

FIND YOUR TRIBE
This takes time, but focus on spending time with those that bring you happiness. With those that **let you be you, those who accept you for who you are** while gently encouraging you to be the best version of you.

Be around those that bring out the best in you and you can bring out the best in them. There is a saying 'iron sharpens iron' **find your tribe that accepts you and also challenges you because they see the greatness in you. They say we are the most like the 5 people we spend the most time with.** There is power in choosing your inner circle wisely as you will eventually rise to the level of those you spend the most time with. Choose positive, supportive people to be in your inner circle.

GIVE BACK TO THE WORLD.
You can create your own happiness by making others happy. There is a true gift in giving. Think of how it feels to wrap a gift and give it to a friend. It is true that the giver receives as much as the receiver.

Also be willing to receive. Many people have a difficult time receiving, whether it is a physical gift, a compliment or an act of kindness. Give yourself permission to receive. It is a gift to you and the other person.

CREATE EXPERIENCES
Having pleasurable and memorable experiences with those you care about creates a deeper and more meaningful connection and enhances your sense of self-worth and joy.

Whether you are creating spur of the moment experiences or planning activities in advance. **Create moments for creating enjoyable experiences and memories.** It may be a mini vacation, a massage, camping or a day trip to the nearest hot spring, exploring activities that **give you a sense of delight.**

Be aware of what and who your energy drainers are. Sometimes we cannot avoid energy drains, but just the simple act of awareness allows you to plan for extra selfcare time to recharge and rejuvenate your body, soul and mind.

LEARN TO SAY 'NO' AND WHEN TO SAY 'YES'.

Boundaries and healthy communication are an integral part of selfcare. Creating healthy boundaries will help you find your own happiness without letting others dictate it for you.

Before saying yes to requests, think about if it's something you really want to do or if it aligns with your values. If it doesn't, politely decline, this is a part of healthy communication and is important for every relationship you have.

BE AWARE

Be aware when the ego mind is creeping in and taking up space in your mind and behaviors. When we let fear, control, and other negative emotions control our minds, ego takes over and causes a disconnect from self and from others. Ask yourself 'is this moving towards connection or away from it?"

SELF-AWARENESS

Selfcare is a self-awareness of what causes a disconnect with yourself and with those around you and giving yourself permission to let go of what is damaging connection. When you feel fear, negativity, jealousy, or even a gossip attitude creep in, stop and ask yourself 'what is happening for me? What do I need right now to create a sense of security and confidence. Finding a safe and comforting place, a place that you feel protected, but where you can also learn from your mistakes without any judgment.

CURIOSITY AND COMPASSION

Have a curiosity and a compassion for yourself. These two words kept in your daily vocabulary in your mind will be a lifeline to your happiness and relationships.

DELIGHT

Find moments for just delighting in life and the beauty around you. Create moments for joy! You are worth it!

"Life is a dance, whatever you do, keep dancing."

REFLECTION

What are your greatest self-care acts that you can schedule into your daily/weekly calendar?

LETTER TO FUTURE SELF.

Picture yourself in 5 years from now. What advice would you like to give yourself in 5 years from now? What goals are you setting now for yourself in 5 years, envision your future and what you are doing, remind yourself of this time and the values and strengths you have. What does the future 'you' need to know in 5 years from now?

Example of a letter written to my older self:

> April 24, 2027
>
> Dear future self,
>
> Wow it is hard to believe that 5 years have flown by so fast. I can hardly believe everything that has happened. Do you remember that time when you questioned who you are? A lot has happened, some of which you hoped for, and some which you didn't dare to dream about at the time. Our family is doing well. The kids are great. It hasn't all been easy but look at the life you have created. You are a confident woman comfortable in your own skin. But I want to remind you to take care of yourself and take time to push the pause button. You have accomplished so many of your goals, I remember how fragile you were when you started on your own. You were so worried all the time, about making a living, about being a good provider, and being a good mom. Remember the funny part is that things picked up when you stopped trying so hard to make it all work. When you focused on the contribution instead – on making things other people found genuinely helpful and useful - all of the other things you wanted flowed from that.
>
> Look at you now, I knew you could achieve your goals and make the impact that you always felt was on your heart to make. You are making a profound difference, offering hope and joy to so many souls. I am so proud of you.
>
> If I have any advice for you, it's this: Breath. Think ten times bigger. A hundred times bigger. Don't limit yourself. Worry less, way less, about mistakes you might make and about what people think or about "who am I to attempt such a thing?" Dare to make a difference. Dare to make a splash. Not for yourself or for your business, but for other people. The world could still use it, maybe now more than ever. Go on a vacation. I know you just got back from one a few months ago but plan your next one and remember how you used to always want to take your children with. Do it again.

Plan a girl's trip. And future self, don't hold onto grudges, but also set healthy boundaries. Say what needs to be said and love with compassion and curiosity. Remember to dance. Those dance lessons you took. You are a great dancer and dance every day. It keeps you young and full of laughter. Keep dreaming.

More than anything, always be you. Let your authentic beautiful you shine. Don't hide who you are and the gifts you have. Be authentically you. Dare to be bold.

With love,
Your younger self,

Write a letter to your future self. Choose a time, 5 years, 10 years, or 20 years. Some people write a letter for 5 years and once they open it and read it in 5 years, they write another letter for their future self.

Dear Future Self,

Chapter 10 | Beautiful Authentic You

REFLECTION
What are your wins today? Ask this question each day as a check-in. It can be easy to forget the accomplishments you make, but the little one's matter as much as the larger ones.

*If this is the second time you were to
live this day, how would you live this day differently?*

Who needs you to be on your A game?

If I was super bold what would life look like?

Is it more painful to keep your true self and all your hopes, dreams, goals and desires locked up inside you because you never unlocked them and let them be seen and got started OR more painful to let the world see the real you, pursue your dreams, experience the journey and possibly fail but know that you gave it everything you had?

The power of the mind is truly amazing. **The more you believe in yourself and who you are as the beautiful inspiring human you are, the more easily and naturally you will reach your goal and dreams and walk in your full identity.**

POWER STATEMENT

The next assignment is an important exercise designed to help you embrace the positive beliefs of who you are.

Use this exercise to push **beyond your comfort zone** and push past the 'do not brag' belief. Today give yourself permission to say it out loud.

Write an exhaustive list of who you are. Include your strengths, talents, education, experiences, characteristics, accomplishments, support systems and anything else you can think of.

Example - I am courageous, I am brave, I am bold, I am pretty, I am strong, I am healthy, I am a great friend, I am supportive.

Use complete 'I' statements and sentences. Write as much as you can think of. Notice your feelings and emotions as you write. Write until you cannot think of anything else to write.

Stop and take a break, come back to your writing and begin again.

Do this 3 times. This serves two purposes. First when you take a break and then come back to your writing, you will be able to go deeper and uncover things that are not right at the surface. Second, as you begin again you will read what you have already written and create a mindset, strengthening your belief in what you have already written.

POWER STATEMENT

Fill in the following blanks to complete your power statement.

I am _____

Your why _____

Example - I am a bold and confident woman empowering and equipping individuals to discover who they are, so they can reach their goals and dreams while living uninhibited with boldness.

Put this statement up somewhere that you can see it every day. Make it your homepage on your phone or computer. Put it on your bathroom mirror with mascara or a dry erase marker. Say it and believe! This is who you are at the core of your being. This is the essence of who you are.

WORDS OF AFFIRMATION:

List 10 people that you trust and ask them to each send you 3 words describing how they see you. Take these words and review them when you feel like you need a self-talk or a kick in the butt.

FINALE

Believe in yourself. You are valuable and worthy. The world needs you to be on your A game! The world needs you to let that light inside you shine bright. The light that you have hidden, continue to let it shine bright as you have begun to do in the last 9 weeks.

You have this one wild and precious life to live...

Will you choose to show up and live this amazing life you have as your true authentic self or wearing a mask of pretense? What Would it be like to embrace the essence of who you are? **What if we dared to embrace our imperfections and quirks and rather looked at these imperfections as a unique gift?**

When you choose to be true to you, you have the power to shift your life and the culture around you.

Brene Brown expresses:

"To be authentic, we must cultivate the courage to be imperfect - and vulnerable. We have to believe that we are fundamentally worthy of love and acceptance, just as we are. I've learned that there is no better way to invite more grace, gratitude and joy into our lives than by mindfully practicing authenticity." "When I choose to be true to me, I have the power to shift my life and my culture around me."

Authenticity promotes connection and authenticity from others. When you choose to show up, to know and embrace what makes you different, you will feel better about yourself, you bring your truest self to your actions and invite others to the same.

When you are real, you are inviting others into realness with you just by being you. There is so much beauty in someone that has put the mask of pretense down and shows up.

Dare! Dare to step outside your comfort zone. Do what scares you

In a movie I watched this one sentence that struck me:

"Why are you trying so hard to fit in when you are born to stand out?"

I am excited for you in the next weeks, months, and years. You will continue to grow where you keep your heart open. **Never forget that you have a purpose on this earth. You are beautiful just the way you are.**

You are loved and so beautifully worthy of love.

"Whatever you can do or dream you can, begin it, Boldness has a genius, power and magic in it. Begin it now"
- Johann Wolfgang Goethe

SELF CARE

Do something for you and for someone you love.

Buy a friend a coffee. Get a massage for yourself. Have a spa night at home with a friend. Read a book in a hot bubble bath with candles. Get away for a night. Spoil yourself and feel loved and worthy.

HOMEWORK

Do something that scares you.

Do something that makes you laugh in delight.

All those words that you have had said about you, those affirmations. Your truth, put them on a wall where you can see them and be constantly reminded every day of your truth.

"You've gotta dance like there's nobody watching, love like you'll never be hurt, sing like there's nobody listening, and live like it's heaven on earth." William W. Purkey

"Don't be afraid to give up the good to go for the great." – John D. Rockefeller

Go out into the world and live as the best and most true version of yourself. Give to the world and shine your brightest. Don't hold your beautiful self-back! You have so much to offer the world, now go and do what makes your heart sing.

Unstoppable - Sia

References
"CliftonStrengths Online Talent Assessment | EN." Gallup, 20 September 2019, www.gallup.com cliftonstrengths. Accessed
22 March 2023.

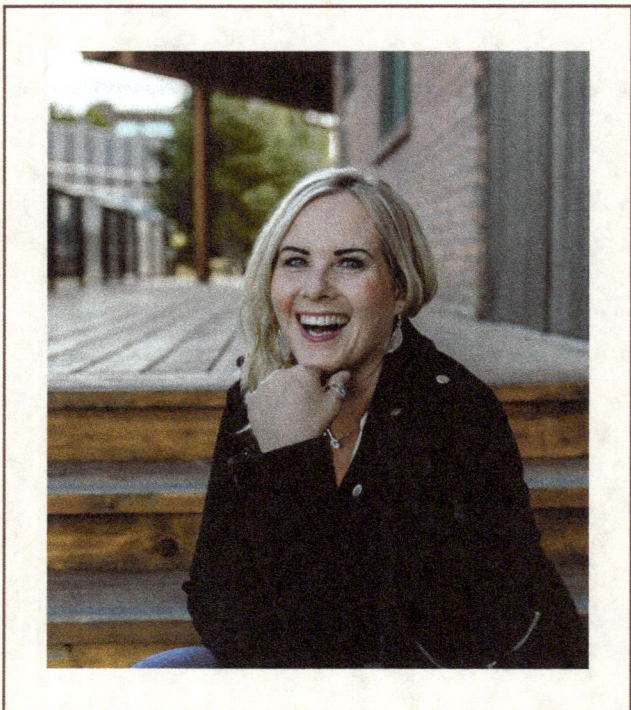

about the author

Ellen Reimer is a Registered Professional Counselor, Personal Life Coach, a mom to 4 men and a woman with a burning desire to see others live life with purpose and zeal, confident in knowing who they are designed and created to be.

Through Ellen's own journey she found that 'growth happens outside the comfort zone' she stepped outside of a life of 'religion within community' to a world unknown with her small family.

She came to understand the importance and freedom in healing pain from the past, embracing her story and becoming the woman God designed her to be.

Ellen's purpose and mission is to see every individual find this freedom, to live with passion, purpose and walk in the love and wisdom of everything that their Creator placed inside each of them.

Throughout this workbook you will find many of the same tools that Ellen used in her own journey of healing and learning. Her desire is for you to also embrace the messiness of life, find healing, forgiveness, joy, confidence and live life with zeal and boldness.

A parallel workbook to 'Unlock Your God-Confidence Workbook' **without** the faith-based / spiritual point of view.

www.ingramcontent.com/pod-product-compliance
Lightning Source LLC
Chambersburg PA
CBHW081114080526
44587CB00021B/3595